# Content Table

## Introduction

Why small business growth is important ___ _02
The challenges of growing a small business ___05
The benefits of a successful growth strategy ___08

## Chapter 1: Assessing Your Business's Growth Potential

Identifying your business's current stage ___03
Analyzing your industry and competition ___07
Identifying opportunities for growth ___10

## Chapter 2: Developing a Growth Plan

Setting measurable growth goals ___16
Identifying the resources required for growth ___21
Prioritizing and implementing growth initiatives ___23

## Chapter 3: Building a Strong Team

Hiring and retaining top talent ___32
Developing a positive company culture ___35
Managing and motivating employee ___40

## Chapter 4: Marketing for Growth

Building a Strong Brand ___48
Developing an effective marketing strategy ___52
Utilizing digital marketing to reach new customers ___54

# Content Table

## Chapter 5: Financing for Growth

Understanding financing options ___ 61
Raising capital for growth ___ 64
Managing financial risks ___ 70

## Chapter 6: Managing Operations for Growth

Streamlining processes and systems ___ 80
Implementing technology solutions ___ 82
Managing inventory and logistics ___ 85

## Chapter 7: Managing Growth Challenges

Dealing with unexpected obstacles ___ 100
Adapting to change ___ 104
Managing stress and burnout ___ 107

## Chapter 8: Case Studies

Success stories of small businesses that have achieved significant growth ___ 114
Lessons learned from their experiences ___ 117

## Conclusion

Summarizing the key takeaways ___ 122
Final thoughts and recommendations ___ 124

Copyright © 2023 by **IMAD BOUTTAN**

All rights reserved.

"Copyright Notice: This book, 'Beyond the Start-Up: A Guide to Small Business Growth,' is copyright protected. The author holds the exclusive rights to reproduce, distribute, and sell the book. No part of this book may be reproduced, stored in a retrieval system, or transmitted in any form or by any means, electronic, mechanical, photocopying, recording, or otherwise, without the prior written permission of the author. Unauthorized reproduction, distribution, or sale of this book is strictly prohibited and punishable by law."

## Disclaimer

The information provided in this book, 'Beyond the Start-Up: A Guide to Small Business Growth,' is for general informational purposes only. The author and publisher make no representations or warranties of any kind, express or implied, about the completeness, accuracy, reliability, suitability or availability with respect to the information, products, services, or related graphics contained in this book for any purpose. Any reliance you place on such information is strictly at your own risk. The author and publisher will not be liable for any errors or omissions, or for any losses, injuries, or damages arising from the use of the information contained in this book. The strategies and information presented in this book may not be suitable for every business, and it is the reader's responsibility to consult with professional advisors before making any business decisions. The case studies presented in this book are specific examples and should not be considered a guarantee of success."

Book Cover by **Imad Bouttan**

Illustrations by **Imad Bouttan**

bouttanimad@gmail.com

[Edition 1] edition [2023]

**INTRODUCTION**

In this book, we will explore the various strategies and tactics that small business owners can use to grow their companies. Small business growth is important for many reasons, from creating jobs and driving economic growth to increasing profitability and creating new opportunities for expansion. However, growing a small business can also be challenging, as small businesses often face unique obstacles that larger companies do not.

In the current business world, small business owners have to be more competitive than ever before. With the rise of digital technology and e-commerce, the market has become more global and more competitive. But this is also a great opportunity for small businesses to stand out and reach new customers.

The goal of this book is to provide small business owners with the tools and insights they need to navigate these challenges and achieve sustainable growth. We will examine a wide range of topics, including assessing your business's growth potential, developing a growth plan, building a strong team, marketing for growth, financing for growth, managing operations, and dealing with growth-related challenges.

We will also provide a detailed analysis of the latest trends and best practices in small business growth. From understanding the key drivers of growth to implementing the right strategies and tactics, this book will give you the knowledge and tools you need to grow your small business successfully.

Throughout the book, we will also share real-world examples and case studies of small businesses that have successfully grown, highlighting the strategies and tactics that have worked for them. By the end of the book, you will have a comprehensive understanding of how to grow your small business and be equipped with the knowledge and tools you need to succeed.

**Why small business growth is important**

Small business growth is essential for the overall health and prosperity of the economy. According to the Small Business Administration, small businesses account for 99.9% of all employers and employ half of all private-sector employees in the United States. This means that when small businesses grow, they create jobs and drive economic growth.

In addition to driving economic growth, small business growth also creates new opportunities for expansion. As small businesses grow, they are able to expand their product or service offerings, enter new markets, and increase their customer base. This not only benefits the business owner, but also the community and the economy as a whole.

Small business growth also leads to increased profitability. As a business grows, it is able to achieve economies of scale and reduce costs. This means that the business can charge lower prices, increase production, and increase profits. Additionally, as a business grows, it is able to take on more employees, which can lead to increased productivity and efficiency.

Finally, small business growth also contributes to innovation and competition. As small businesses grow, they are able to invest in new technology, research and development, and product development. This leads to new and improved products and services, which in turn leads to increased competition and innovation in the market.

In conclusion, the health and success of the economy as a whole depend on small company growth. It boosts employment and economic growth, opens up new business prospects, increases profitability, and fosters innovation and competitiveness. Small business owners must therefore prioritize growth and devise plans to realize it.

Warby Parker is one actual case of a small business that has seen enormous growth. Four friends launched the American eyewear business Warby Parker in 2010. The company's goal is to address the global problem of limited access to glasses while also offering fashionable, reasonably priced eyewear.

In the early days, Warby Parker sold their glasses primarily through their website and pop-up stores. However, as the company grew, it began to expand its brick-and-mortar presence, opening physical stores across the United States. Today, the company has over 100 retail locations in the United States and Canada.

One of the key strategies that Warby Parker used to achieve growth was to focus on providing exceptional customer service. The company built a strong reputation for providing high-quality products and exceptional customer service. As a result, it was able to attract new customers and retain its existing ones.

Another strategy that Warby Parker used to achieve growth was to focus on innovation. The company invested in research and development to create new and improved products, which helped to increase its market share and attract new customers.

Finally, Warby Parker also focused on building a strong brand. The company used a variety of marketing strategies, including social media, online advertising, and public relations, to increase brand awareness and attract new customers.

In general, Warby Parker's success may be due to its emphasis on delivering top-notch customer service, making investments in innovation, and forging a credible brand. The company has experienced substantial growth as a result of this strategy, and it is now a key force in the eyeglasses sector.

## The challenges of growing a small business

Growing a small business can be a challenging and complex process, requiring a great deal of time, effort, and resources. There are a number of obstacles that small business owners must navigate in order to achieve sustainable growth. In this article, we will examine some of the most common challenges of growing a small business.

One of the biggest challenges of growing a small business is financing. Small businesses often struggle to access the capital they need to invest in growth initiatives. This can include everything from buying inventory, to hiring new employees, to expanding into new markets. Without adequate financing, small businesses may find it difficult to take advantage of growth opportunities.

Another major challenge of growing a small business is managing cash flow. As a business grows, it often requires more money to meet increased demand for products and services. This can lead to cash flow problems, as the business may not have enough money on hand to meet its obligations. This can lead to financial difficulties and can even put the business at risk of failure.

A third challenge of growing a small business is building a strong team. As a business grows, it often requires more employees to meet increased demand for products and services. However, finding and retaining top talent can be difficult. This can be especially true for small businesses that may not have the resources to compete with larger companies for top talent.

Another challenge of growing a small business is managing risk. As a business grows, it often takes on more risk. This can include everything from financial risks to operational risks to market risks. If not properly managed, these risks can lead to significant losses and even put the business at risk of failure.

Finally, growing a small business often requires significant changes to the way the business operates. This can include everything from changes to processes and systems to changes to the organizational structure. Making these changes can be difficult and can lead to resistance from employees and other stakeholders.

In conclusion, growing a small business is a challenging and complex process that requires a great deal of time, effort, and resources. Small business owners must navigate a number of obstacles in order to achieve sustainable growth. These obstacles include financing, cash flow, building a strong team, managing risk, and making significant changes to the way the business operates. By understanding these challenges, small business owners can better prepare themselves to navigate the challenges of growth and achieve success.

The bakery "Sweet Treats Bakery" is an illustration of a tiny company that has encountered difficulties as it expanded. Sarah, the proprietor, launched the company in her kitchen at home using only a few simple baking materials and her love of baking. She started off by hawking her baked goods at neighborhood farmers markets, quickly establishing a name for her delectable cakes and pastries.

As the business grew, Sarah realized that she needed to expand her kitchen and purchase more baking equipment to keep up with demand. However, she struggled to secure financing from banks and other traditional lenders to make these investments. This was a major challenge for her and she had to look for alternative ways to finance her business-like crowdfunding, asking for a loan from family and friends, and even taking a personal loan.

Another challenge that Sarah faced was managing cash flow. As the business grew, she had to purchase more ingredients and equipment, which increased her expenses. However, her revenue was not increasing at the same pace, which led to cash flow problems. She had to negotiate with suppliers for better payment terms, and even had to delay some payments to keep her business running.

As the business continued to grow, Sarah also faced a challenge in building a strong team. She struggled to find and retain skilled bakers and other staff, as she couldn't offer the same salary and benefits as larger bakeries. She had to be creative in her recruitment strategies and even trained some of her employees herself.

Finally, as her company expanded, Sarah had to tackle the difficulty of risk management. She had to manage the dangers of starting a retail business and deal with food safety laws. She had to spend money on insurance and employ a consultant to guide her through the rules.

Generally, there were difficulties in the growth of Sweet Treats Bakery. Sarah had to overcome challenges like funding, cash flow, assembling a capable team, and risk management. However, she overcame these obstacles and expanded her company into a prosperous bakery with tenacity and diligence.

**The benefits of business growth**

Business growth is a process that can bring a wide range of benefits to companies of all sizes. Whether you're a small business owner or the CEO of a large corporation, growth can help to drive success and create new opportunities. In this article, we'll explore some of the key benefits of business growth.

One of the most obvious benefits of business growth is increased revenue. As a business grows, it is able to sell more products or services, which leads to increased revenue. This can help to improve the bottom line, create new opportunities for expansion, and support ongoing operations.

Another benefit of business growth is increased profitability. As a business grows, it can achieve economies of scale, which can help to reduce costs and increase profits. This can also help to create a more sustainable business model, which can support long-term growth and success.

Business growth can also lead to increased competitiveness. As a business grows, it can invest in new technology, research and development, and product development. This can help to create new and improved products and services, which in turn can lead to increased competition and innovation in the market.

Growing a business can also led to increased employment opportunities. As a business grows, it may require more employees to meet increased demand for products and services. This can help to create jobs and support local economies.

Finally, business growth can also lead to increased brand recognition and awareness. As a business grows, it can invest in marketing and advertising to increase brand awareness and attract new customers. This can help to establish a strong brand, which can be a powerful asset for a business.

In conclusion, businesses of all sizes can profit greatly from company expansion. Growth can contribute to success and open up new prospects through improved income, profitability, competitiveness, and employment chances. Focusing on expansion can promote your long-term success, whether you're the CEO of a major firm or a small business.

One real-life example of a business that has experienced significant growth is the company "Zoom". Zoom is a video conferencing platform that was founded in 2011. The company began as a provider of video conferencing solutions for businesses, but as the company grew, it expanded its offerings to include webinars, online meetings, and video webcasting.

One of the key benefits of Zoom's growth was increased revenue. As the company grew, it was able to sell more of its video conferencing solutions, which led to increased revenue. This allowed the company to invest in new technology and expand its offerings, which in turn helped to drive further growth.

Another benefit of Zoom's growth was increased profitability. As the company grew, it was able to achieve economies of scale, which helped to reduce costs and increase profits. This allowed the company to invest in new technologies and expand its offerings, which helped to drive further growth.

Zoom's growth also led to increased competitiveness. As the company grew, it invested in new technology and expanded its offerings. This helped to create new and improved products and services, which in turn led to increased competition and innovation in the video conferencing market.

Finally, Zoom's growth also led to increased brand recognition and awareness. As the company grew, it invested in marketing and advertising to increase brand awareness and attract new customers. This helped to establish Zoom as a leading player in the video conferencing market and helped to drive further growth.

Overall, Zoom's growth brought a wide range of benefits to the company, including increased revenue, profitability, competitiveness, and brand recognition. By focusing on growth, Zoom has become a major player in the video conferencing market and continues to experience significant growth.

CHAPTER 1

# Assessing Your Business's Growth Potential

Assessing your business's growth potential is an essential step in achieving sustainable growth. It involves identifying your business's current stage, analyzing your industry and competition, and identifying opportunities for growth. By taking the time to assess your business's growth potential, you can gain a better understanding of where your business stands and identify opportunities for growth.

The first step in assessing your business's growth potential is identifying your business's current stage. This involves evaluating where your business stands in terms of size, revenue, and market share. This can help you understand the potential for growth and identify any areas that need improvement. For example, a business that is just starting out will have a different growth potential than a business that has been established for several years.

The next step is analyzing your industry and competition. This involves researching your industry and competition to identify trends, strengths, and weaknesses. This can help you understand the market conditions and identify opportunities for growth. For example, if you are in a growing industry, your business may have a greater potential for growth than if you were in a declining industry. Understanding your competition and their strengths and weaknesses can also help you identify areas where your business can differentiate itself and potentially gain a competitive advantage.

The final step is identifying opportunities for growth. This involves identifying areas where your business can expand, such as new markets, products or services, or geographic regions. It also involves evaluating the potential for growth in these areas and determining if the potential benefits outweigh the risks. For example, if you identify an opportunity to enter a new market, you will need to evaluate the potential for growth in that market and determine if the potential benefits outweigh the costs and risks of entering that market.

Assessing your business's growth potential can be a complex process, but it is essential for achieving sustainable growth. It is important to consider not only the market conditions but also the company's own resources and capacity to absorb the growth. This process should be an ongoing one, as the market, industry and the company itself will change and evolve over time. By taking the time to assess your business's growth potential, you can develop a growth plan and take the necessary steps to achieve sustainable growth for your company.

**Identifying your business's current stage**

Identifying the current stage of your business is crucial for determining the appropriate strategies and actions to take in order to achieve your goals. There are typically four stages of a business: startup, growth, maturity, and decline. Understanding which stage your business is in can help you make informed decisions about everything from marketing and sales to operations and finances.

**Startup stage:** This is the beginning phase of a business, where an entrepreneur develops and tests a new product or service. At this stage, the business is focused on creating a viable product or service, and building a customer base. The main goal of this stage is to validate the market and the business model. The startup stage is characterized by high uncertainty, limited resources, and a small customer base.

**Growth stage:** After a business has validated its market and business model, it enters the growth stage. During this stage, the business is focused on scaling operations, increasing revenue and growing the customer base. This is a critical stage for a business, as it can make or break the company. The main goal of this stage is to increase revenue and achieve profitability. The growth stage is characterized by increased competition, increased demand for the product or service, and a need for additional resources.

**Maturity stage:** Once a business has achieved profitability, it enters the maturity stage. During this stage, the business is focused on maintaining market share and maximizing profits. The main goal of this stage is to optimize operations, streamline processes and maintain customer loyalty. The maturity stage is characterized by slow growth, increased competition, and a focus on cost-cutting measures.

**Decline stage:** As a business reaches the end of its life cycle, it enters the decline stage. During this stage, the business is focused on liquidating assets and closing down operations. The main goal of this stage is to minimize losses and return as much value to shareholders as possible. The decline stage is characterized by decreasing revenue, increasing costs, and a decrease in customer demand.

In order to identify the current stage of your business, you should analyze the market, your competition, and your financial performance.

You should also consider factors such as the rate of growth, customer demand, and the level of competition in your industry. By taking the time to identify the current stage of your business, you can make informed decisions about how to move forward and achieve your goals.

A real-life example of a business that has gone through the different stages of its life cycle is the company Starbucks.

In the startup stage, Starbucks began as a small coffee shop in Seattle in 1971. The company was focused on creating a unique and high-quality coffee experience for customers. The main goal of this stage was to validate the market for specialty coffee.

In the growth stage, Starbucks began to expand rapidly, opening new stores and building a strong customer base. The company's main goal during this stage was to increase revenue and achieve profitability. Starbucks also started to experiment with new products, such as Frappuccinos, and expanded internationally. This stage is characterized by increased demand for their product and high growth rate.

In the maturity stage, Starbucks has become a dominant player in the coffee industry, with thousands of stores worldwide. The company's main goal during this stage is to maintain market share and maximize profits. Starbucks started to focus on optimizing operations and streamlining processes, introducing new technologies like mobile ordering and delivery. They also started to focus on customer loyalty by introducing reward program and loyalty card. This stage is characterized by slow growth, increased competition, and a focus on cost-cutting measures.

Starbucks is currently in the maturity stage, with a solid customer base and a well-established brand. The company continues to focus on expanding its product offerings, such as introducing new food items, and leveraging technology to improve the customer experience.

This real-life example of Starbucks illustrates how a business can go through the different stages of its life cycle and how the strategies and goals of the company change as it moves through each stage.

In recent years, Starbucks has started to focus on sustainability and social responsibility initiatives, such as reducing its environmental footprint and supporting local communities. They also started to focus on digital transformation, by introducing new technologies such as mobile app, online ordering and delivery. These initiatives are part of Starbucks' growth strategy as the company looks to continue its expansion and reach new customers.

In addition, Starbucks has also been actively expanding its presence in the Chinese market, which is one of the most important and fast-growing markets in the world. The company has been investing heavily in the market, opening new stores and expanding its product offerings to cater to the local taste.

In essence, Starbucks' ability to effectively navigate the various stages of its life cycle may be attributed to its constant innovation, growth, and market-specific adaptation. The secret to the company's continued success has been its ability to recognize its current stage and modify its plans accordingly.

**Analyzing your industry and competition**

Analyzing your industry and competition is essential for any business looking to succeed in today's competitive marketplace. By understanding the industry landscape, a business can identify opportunities, threats, and trends that can inform strategy, operations, and decision-making.

When analyzing your industry, it is important to consider the following factors:

**Industry structure:** This includes the size and growth rate of the industry, the number of players, and their market share. Understanding the structure of your industry can help you identify potential opportunities and threats, as well as the level of competition you can expect.

**Industry trends:** It is important to keep an eye on the latest trends and developments in your industry. This includes technological advancements, changes in consumer behavior, and shifts in regulations. Understanding these trends can help you identify opportunities to innovate and stay ahead of the competition.

**Industry profitability:** Analyzing the profitability of your industry can help you understand the potential for growth and the level of investment required to succeed. It can also help you identify opportunities to reduce costs and increase efficiency.

When analyzing your competition, it is important to consider the following factors:

**Market share:** Understanding the market share of your competitors can help you identify the leaders in your industry and the level of competition you can expect.

**Competitive advantage:** Analyzing the competitive advantage of your competitors can help you understand what sets them apart and how you can differentiate yourself.

**Weaknesses:** Identifying the weaknesses of your competitors can help you identify opportunities to gain market share and outperform them.

Once you have gathered information about your industry and competition, it is important to use this information to inform your business strategy. This can include identifying new opportunities, developing a unique value proposition, and investing in differentiating capabilities. It can also include developing a plan to mitigate potential threats and capitalize on industry trends.

In summary, analyzing your industry and competition is essential for any business looking to succeed in today's competitive marketplace. By understanding the industry landscape and the competitive dynamics, a business can make informed decisions and develop effective strategies to achieve its goals.

Patagonia is a real-world illustration of a business that has effectively assessed its industry and rivals.

Patagonia is an outdoor clothing and gear company that was founded in 1973. The company's mission is to create high-quality, sustainable products while also promoting environmental activism.

In analyzing its industry, Patagonia recognized that the outdoor clothing and gear market was highly competitive, with many large players such as The North Face and Columbia. However, the company also recognized that there was a growing demand for sustainable and ethically-made products. By focusing on these areas, Patagonia was able to differentiate itself from its competitors and tap into a niche market.

In terms of competition, Patagonia has always been aware of its larger competitors, but it has also focused on building a loyal customer base through its commitment to sustainability and environmental activism. For example, the company has invested in sustainable materials and production methods, and it actively promotes environmental conservation through its various initiatives such as 1% for the Planet. By doing so, Patagonia has been able to build a strong brand and a loyal customer base, which has helped it to maintain its market share and profitability.

Patagonia is a business that has successfully studied its sector and rivals, discovered a niche market and set itself apart via its dedication to sustainability and environmental activism. This has aided the business in maintaining its competitive edge and achieving long-term success.

**Identifying opportunities for growth**

Any company wishing to grow and succeed over the long run must first identify growth possibilities. A company can boost revenue, boost efficiency, and maintain an edge over the competition by discovering new markets, products, or client groups.

When identifying opportunities for growth, it is important to consider the following factors:

**Market trends:** Keep an eye on the latest trends and developments in your industry. This includes technological advancements, changes in consumer behavior, and shifts in regulations. Understanding these trends can help you identify new opportunities for growth.

**Customer needs:** Understand the needs of your current and potential customers. This includes identifying unmet needs and pain points that your business can address. By addressing these needs, you can increase customer satisfaction and loyalty.

**Competitor analysis:** Analyze your competition and identify areas where they are weak or under-serving the market. This can help you identify opportunities to gain market share and outperform them.

Once you have identified opportunities for growth, it is important to develop a plan to capitalize on them. This can include developing new products or services, entering new markets, or expanding your customer base.

For example, a real-life company that has successfully identified opportunities for growth is Peloton. Peloton is a technology-enabled fitness company that started with a focus on indoor cycling. However, over time the company realized that there was a huge opportunity to expand into other fitness segments. Peloton identified the trend of people wanting to workout at home and the rise of streaming workout classes. By capitalizing on this opportunity, Peloton expanded its product offerings to include a variety of workout types, such as yoga and strength training. This has helped the company to attract a wider customer base and increase revenue.

In conclusion, locating growth prospects is an essential step for every company seeking to develop and experience long-term success. A firm can create a strategy to take advantage of new chances and accomplish its objectives by comprehending market trends, client wants, and competitor analyses.

Netflix is another real-life example of a company that has successfully identified opportunities for growth. When Netflix first started, it was primarily a mail-order DVD rental service. However, the company quickly realized that the potential for growth in the streaming industry was huge. By analyzing market trends and customer needs, Netflix identified the opportunity to pivot to a streaming-based model. By capitalizing on this opportunity, Netflix expanded its product offerings to include original content, and it started to stream movies and TV shows online. This has helped the company to attract a wider customer base and increase revenue.

Another real-life example of a company that has successfully identified opportunities for growth is the organic food company, Whole Foods. When the company first started, its focus was on providing organic and natural food products to health-conscious consumers. However, over time Whole Foods realized that there was a growing demand for organic and natural food products among a wider customer base. By capitalizing on this opportunity, Whole Foods expanded its product offerings to include more conventional products. The company also began to focus on reducing prices and increasing accessibility, which helped it to attract a wider customer base and increase revenue. Whole Foods also had the opportunity to diversify their market by expanding their e-commerce and delivery options, making the access to their products even more convenient for consumers.

In both examples, Netflix and Whole Foods, the companies have been able to successfully identify opportunities for growth and capitalize on them by adapting to changing market conditions and customer needs. This has helped them to achieve long-term success and become leaders in their respective industries.

CHAPTER 2

# Developing a Growth Plan

Developing a growth plan is an essential step for any business looking to expand and achieve long-term success. A growth plan is a comprehensive document that outlines the strategies, actions, and resources needed to achieve specific growth objectives. By developing a growth plan, a business can identify new opportunities, set clear goals, and allocate resources effectively.

*The following steps should be taken into account while creating a growth plan:*

**Identify opportunities:** The first step in developing a growth plan is to identify opportunities for growth. This includes analyzing market trends, customer needs, and competitor analysis to identify areas where the business can expand.

**Set clear goals:** Once opportunities for growth have been identified, the next step is to set clear and measurable goals. These goals should be specific, time-bound, and aligned with the overall vision of the business.

**Develop strategies:** Based on the goals set, develop strategies to achieve them. These strategies should be specific, actionable and aligned with the overall vision of the business.

**Allocate resources:** After strategies have been developed, it is important to allocate the necessary resources to implement them. This includes financial, human, and technological resources.

**Monitor progress:** Regularly monitor the progress of the growth plan, and adjust strategies and resources as needed.

Review and Revise: Review the plan regularly and revise it as needed based on the progress and any changes in the market.

For example, a real-life example of a company that has successfully developed a growth plan is the mobile app company, Uber. When Uber first launched, its focus was on providing a ride-hailing service in select cities. However, the company quickly realized that the potential for growth in the transportation industry was huge. By developing a growth plan, Uber was able to identify new opportunities, such as expanding into new markets, developing new services, and leveraging technology to improve the customer experience. As a result, the company has grown rapidly and become a global leader in the transportation industry.

To sum, creating a growth plan is a crucial step for any company hoping to grow and experience long-term success. A company can accomplish its growth goals and enjoy long-term success by identifying opportunities, setting specific goals, devising strategies, assigning resources, monitoring progress, and reviewing and amending the plan.

**Setting measurable growth goals**

Setting measurable growth goals is an essential part of any business or organization's success. These goals provide a clear direction for the company and its employees, and they also serve as a benchmark for measuring progress and success. Without measurable growth goals, it can be difficult to know if a business is on track to meet its objectives and achieve its desired level of success.

There are several different types of growth goals that a company can set, including financial goals, customer acquisition goals, and employee performance goals. Financial goals are perhaps the most straightforward type of growth goal, as they involve setting targets for revenue, profit, or other financial metrics. For example, a company may set a goal to increase its revenue by 20% over the next year, or to achieve a certain level of profit margin.

Customer acquisition goals are another important type of growth goal, as they focus on attracting new customers to the business. These goals can include targets for the number of new customers acquired, as well as metrics such as customer lifetime value and customer retention rate. For example, a company may set a goal to acquire a certain number of new customers each month, or to increase its customer retention rate by a certain percentage.

Employee performance goals are also important, as they focus on the development and performance of the company's workforce. These goals can include targets for employee productivity, engagement, and retention, as well as metrics such as employee turnover rate and employee satisfaction. For example, a company may set a goal to reduce its employee turnover rate by a certain percentage, or to increase employee engagement and satisfaction by a certain amount.

When setting measurable growth goals, it is important to ensure that the goals are specific, measurable, achievable, relevant, and time-bound (SMART). Specific goals are those that are clearly defined and easy to understand. Measurable goals are those that can be quantified and tracked. Achievable goals are those that are realistic and possible to achieve. Relevant goals are those that align with the company's overall objectives and mission. Time-bound goals are those that have a specific deadline for completion.

In addition to setting measurable growth goals, it is also important to establish a system for tracking progress and measuring success. This can involve creating a dashboard or other tool for tracking key performance indicators (KPIs) and progress against goals. It can also involve regularly reviewing progress and making adjustments as needed.

In inevitable conclusion, establishing quantifiable growth targets is crucial to the success of any company or organization. These objectives serve as a guide for the business and its personnel as well as a yardstick for gauging development and success. It is crucial to make sure that your growth goals are time-bound, relevant, measurable, and explicit. Additionally, it's crucial to set up a system for monitoring success and tracking progress, reviewing progress frequently, and making adjustments as necessary. This will make sure that the business is on pace to accomplish its goals and succeed to the required degree.

A real-life simulation of setting measurable growth goals might look something like this:

1. Assess current performance: Begin by conducting a thorough analysis of the company's current performance, including financial metrics, customer acquisition, and employee performance. This will provide a baseline for setting growth goals and measuring progress.

2. Identify areas for improvement: Based on the assessment of current performance, identify areas where the company needs to improve in order to achieve its desired level of success. These areas will become the focus of the growth goals.

3. Set specific, measurable, achievable, relevant and time-bound (SMART) goals: For each area identified in step 2, set specific, measurable, achievable, relevant, and time-bound goals. For example, a financial goal might be to increase revenue by 20% over the next year, while a customer acquisition goal might be to acquire a certain number of new customers each month.

4. Develop a plan of action: For each growth goal, develop a plan of action that outlines the steps that will be taken to achieve the goal. This plan should include specific actions and milestones, as well as a timeline for completion.

5. Assign responsibilities: Assign specific individuals or teams within the company to be responsible for achieving each growth goal. This will ensure that the goals are being actively worked on and that progress is being tracked.

6. Track progress and measure success: Set up a system for tracking progress against each goal and measuring success. This might include creating a dashboard or other tool for tracking key performance indicators (KPIs) or conducting regular reviews of progress.

7. Review and adjust as needed: Regularly review progress against each goal and make adjustments as needed. This might involve modifying the plan of action, reassigning responsibilities, or setting new goals.

8. Celebrate Success: Once goals are achieved, celebrate the success and acknowledge the team members who worked hard to achieve the goals. This will motivate the team and encourage them to achieve more.

Remembering that creating growth goals is a continuous activity rather than a one-time event is crucial. The objectives should evolve together with the company. Additionally, it's critical to be adaptable and change the goals as necessary in response to the company's success and outside influences.

**Identifying the resources required for growth**

Identifying the resources required for growth is a critical step in the process of setting and achieving measurable growth goals. Without a clear understanding of the resources that are needed, a company may struggle to achieve its desired level of success. Resources can include a wide range of items such as financial, human, technology and other resources.

Financial resources are perhaps the most obvious type of resource needed for growth. These include funds for investments in new equipment, technology, and research and development. In order to identify the financial resources required for growth, a company should conduct a thorough analysis of its current financial situation and create a detailed budget that outlines the funds that will be required to achieve its growth goals. This budget should take into account not only the costs of achieving the goals, but also the potential return on investment.

Human resources are also an essential component of growth. A company's workforce is a valuable asset and plays a critical role in its success. Identifying the human resources required for growth involves assessing the company's current workforce and determining the skills and experience that are needed to achieve the growth goals. This may involve recruiting new employees with the necessary skills and experience, or training and developing existing employees to meet the needs of the company.

Technology is another important resource for growth. As technology is changing so fast, it's important to stay ahead of the game. Many companies rely on technology to drive their operations, and identifying the technology resources required for growth may involve investing in new software and hardware, or upgrading existing systems. It's important to ensure that the technology being used is up-to-date and can support the company's growth goals.

Other resources, such as physical space, equipment, and materials, may also be required for growth. For example, a company that is expanding its operations may need to invest in additional equipment and materials, or lease more space. Identifying these resources will help the company understand what it needs to invest in to achieve its growth goals.

Once the resources required for growth have been identified, it's important to prioritize them and make a plan to acquire them. This plan should include timelines and milestones, as well as a budget for acquiring the resources. It's also important to make sure that the resources are being used effectively and efficiently.

In addition to identifying the resources required for growth, it's also important to anticipate and plan for potential roadblocks and challenges that may arise. This may include creating a contingency plan for unexpected events, such as a downturn in the economy or a shift in the market.

Conclusion based, creating and accomplishing quantifiable development goals requires a number of steps, one of which is determining the resources needed for growth. Financial, human, technological, and other resources are all examples of resources. A business should analyze its current condition in depth and develop a thorough budget that specifies the resources needed to meet its growth objectives. Technology and human resources are also crucial elements of growth. Prioritizing resources is crucial, as is creating a plan to acquire them and ensuring their effective and efficient usage. The company will be more successful if potential obstacles and difficulties, such as unforeseen circumstances, are anticipated and planned for.

**Prioritizing and implementing growth initiatives**

Prioritizing and implementing growth initiatives is a crucial step in achieving measurable growth goals for a business or organization. With limited resources and time, it is essential to focus on the initiatives that will have the greatest impact on the company's success.

The first step in prioritizing and implementing growth initiatives is to conduct a thorough analysis of the company's current situation and identify areas for improvement. This may include analyzing financial performance, customer acquisition, employee engagement and retention, and other key performance indicators (KPIs). Once these areas have been identified, the company can set specific, measurable, achievable, relevant, and time-bound (SMART) growth goals.

The next step is to develop a list of potential growth initiatives that could help the company achieve its goals. These initiatives may include expanding into new markets, launching new products or services, increasing marketing and advertising efforts, or improving operations and processes. It's important to consider both short-term and long-term initiatives, as well as those that have a high potential return on investment (ROI) and those that align with the company's overall mission and values.

Once a list of potential growth initiatives has been developed, it's important to prioritize them based on their potential impact, feasibility, and alignment with the company's overall goals. This can be done by using a prioritization matrix or a decision-making framework. Factors to consider when prioritizing initiatives might include the potential impact on revenue, customer acquisition, or employee engagement, as well as the resources required and the potential risks and challenges involved.

Once the growth initiatives have been prioritized, the company can begin to implement them. This may involve creating a detailed plan of action that includes timelines, milestones, and specific responsibilities for each initiative. It's important to allocate the necessary resources, such as funding, personnel, and technology, to ensure that the initiatives are implemented successfully.

Implementing growth initiatives also involves regularly monitoring progress and making adjustments as needed. This may include tracking key performance indicators (KPIs), conducting regular reviews, and making adjustments to the plan of action. It's also important to be flexible and adjust the initiatives as needed based on the company's performance and external factors.

A critical element in accomplishing measurable growth objectives for a firm or organization is identifying and carrying out growth projects. It's crucial to perform a thorough analysis of the business's current state and pinpoint areas for improvement, set specific, measurable, achievable, relevant, and time-bound (SMART) growth goals, develop a list of potential growth initiatives, prioritize them, create a comprehensive action plan, allot the necessary resources, and regularly monitor progress, making adjustments as necessary. This will ensure that the business is concentrating on the projects that will have the biggest influence on its success and that it can meet its growth objectives in a timely and effective manner.

It's important to note that these are just examples and the specific initiatives, goals and the way to measure success may vary depending on the company and its specific needs. Also, the process of setting and achieving measurable growth goals is an ongoing process and not a one-time event. As the company grows, the goals and initiatives will need to be adjusted accordingly.

**A retail store looking to increase revenue**

Simulation:

1. The retail store conducts an analysis of its current performance and identifies that revenue has been stagnant over the past year.
2. The store sets a specific, measurable, achievable, relevant and time-bound (SMART) goal to increase revenue by 15% over the next six months.
3. The store then develops a list of potential growth initiatives, such as launching new products, increasing marketing and advertising efforts, and improving customer service.

4. After prioritizing the initiatives, the store decides to focus on launching new products and increasing marketing and advertising efforts.

5. The store creates a detailed plan of action that includes timelines, milestones, and specific responsibilities for each initiative. This includes allocating funds for product development and marketing campaigns.

6. The store also tracks key performance indicators (KPIs) such as revenue, customer acquisition, and customer satisfaction to measure progress and success.

7. After six months, the store reviews its progress and finds that it has achieved its goal of increasing revenue by 15%.

**A technology company looking to improve employee engagement**

Simulation:

1. The technology company conducts an analysis of its current performance and identifies that employee engagement has been low.

2. The company sets a specific, measurable, achievable, relevant and time-bound (SMART) goal to increase employee engagement by 20% over the next year.

3. The company then develops a list of potential growth initiatives, such as improving employee training and development programs,

increasing communication and transparency, and creating a more collaborative work environment.

4. After prioritizing the initiatives, the company decides to focus on improving employee training and development programs and increasing communication and transparency.

5. The company creates a detailed plan of action that includes timelines, milestones, and specific responsibilities for each initiative. This includes allocating funds for training programs and hiring a new employee engagement manager.

6. The company also tracks key performance indicators (KPIs) such as employee engagement, turnover rate, and satisfaction to measure progress and success.

7. After one year, the company reviews its progress and finds that it has achieved its goal of increasing employee engagement by 20%.

One example of a known African company that has achieved measurable growth in recent years is Jumia, an e-commerce platform that operates in several African countries.

Jumia was founded in 2012 and initially faced challenges in building a reliable logistics network and convincing customers to trust online shopping in Africa. However, the company was able to overcome these challenges by implementing several growth initiatives.

One of the initiatives was to improve the company's logistics and delivery services. Jumia invested in building its own logistics network and also partnered with local and international courier companies to offer more reliable and faster delivery services. This helped to increase customer satisfaction and trust in the platform.

Another initiative was to expand its product offerings, Jumia started to offer a wide range of products such as electronics, fashion, home appliances, and groceries, to attract a wider range of customers and increase its revenue.

The company also focused on building its brand awareness through marketing campaigns and partnerships with popular brands and influencers. This helped to increase its visibility and attract more customers to the platform.

Jumia's efforts paid off, and the company was able to achieve significant growth in recent years. As of 2021, Jumia has over 3 million active customers and is considered one of the most successful e-commerce platforms in Africa.

It's worth noting that Jumia faced a lot of challenges along the way, such as regulatory and operational issues, but they were able to overcome them by being flexible and adjusting their strategy when needed.

CHAPTER 3

# Building a Strong Team

Building a strong team is essential for the success of any organization. A team that works well together can accomplish more than a group of individuals working independently. However, building a strong team is not always easy and requires effort, communication, and commitment from all members.

The first step in building a strong team is to clearly define the goals and objectives of the team. This will ensure that everyone is working towards the same end goal and will prevent confusion and misunderstandings. It is also important to establish clear roles

responsibilities for each team member, so that everyone knows what is expected of them and can work together more effectively.

Effective communication is also crucial for building a strong team. Team members should be encouraged to openly share their ideas, opinions, and concerns. Clear, open, and honest communication helps to build trust and understanding among team members, and allows for more effective problem solving and decision making.

Another important aspect of building a strong team is to foster a positive and supportive work environment. Team members should be encouraged to work together and support one another, rather than competing against each other. This can be achieved by creating a culture of cooperation and mutual respect.

In addition to fostering a positive work environment, it is important to provide opportunities for team members to develop their skills and knowledge. This can be achieved through training and development programs, as well as mentoring and coaching. By investing in the professional growth of team members, organizations can build a more skilled and capable team.

Last but not least, it's critical to thank and honor team members for their accomplishments. Celebrate accomplishments as a team and express gratitude for the team members' efforts. Team members will be more motivated and will have higher levels of morale as a result, which will motivate them to keep working hard and pursue success.

building a strong team is essential for the success of any organization. It requires clear goals and objectives, effective communication, a positive and supportive work environment, opportunities for skill development, and recognition and rewards for hard work. By following these principles, organizations can build a team that is capable of achieving great things.

**Hiring and retaining top talent**

For every organization to succeed, top talent must be attracted and kept. Top talent can bring new ideas, skills, and perspectives that can drive growth and innovation. However, finding and keeping top talent can be a challenging task, and requires a strategic approach.

The first step in hiring top talent is to clearly define the skills, qualifications, and experience that are required for the position. This will ensure that the organization is looking for the right candidates and will help to attract the best possible candidates. It is also important to have a clear and compelling job description that accurately reflects the role and the organization's culture.

The next step is to create an effective recruiting strategy that will reach the right candidates. This may include leveraging social media and professional networks, attending job fairs and industry events, and working with recruitment agencies. It is also important to have a strong employer brand that reflects the organization's values and mission, as this can help to attract top talent.

Once top talent has been identified and recruited, it is important to retain them. One of the key ways to do this is to create a positive and supportive work environment that encourages employee engagement and job satisfaction. This can be achieved by providing opportunities for professional development, promoting work-life balance, and fostering a culture of open communication and teamwork.

Another important aspect of retaining top talent is to provide competitive compensation and benefits packages. This includes not only salary, but also things such as health insurance, retirement plans, and other perks. Additionally, rewarding and recognizing the contributions of employees is essential to keeping them engaged and motivated.

Another important aspect of hiring and retaining top talent is to invest in employee development. By providing opportunities for skill development, education, and training, organizations can help to improve the skills and knowledge of their employees, which can lead to increased job satisfaction and improved performance. it is important to be open to feedback and to respond to the concerns and suggestions of employees. By actively listening to employees, organizations can identify and address issues that may be causing dissatisfaction and prevent top talent from leaving.

Hiring and retaining top talent is essential for the success of any organization. It requires a clear understanding of the skills and qualifications needed, an effective recruiting strategy, a positive and supportive work environment, competitive compensation and benefits, opportunities for skill development, and a culture of open communication and feedback. By following these principles, organizations can build a team of top talent that will drive growth and innovation.

Google, for example, is known for its ability to attract and retain top talent. The company has built a reputation as a leader in technology and innovation, which helps to attract top talent in the industry. Additionally, Google offers competitive compensation and benefits packages, as well as opportunities for professional development and growth. The company also fosters a positive and supportive work environment, which encourages employee engagement and job satisfaction. This is evident in the high retention rate of the employees.

Zappos, on the other hand, an online shoe and clothing store, has built a reputation for its unique company culture and commitment to customer service. The company places a strong emphasis on employee empowerment and encourages employees to take ownership of their roles and responsibilities. Zappos also offers a wide range of benefits and perks, such as free gym membership, flexible working hours and opportunities for professional development. These factors have helped the company to attract and retain top talent, and has a reputation for being an employer of choice in the industry.

**Developing a positive company culture**

Developing a positive company culture is essential for the success of any organization. A positive culture can help to attract and retain top talent, improve employee engagement and productivity, and drive growth and innovation. However, developing a positive culture is not always easy and requires effort and commitment from all members of the organization.

The first step in developing a positive company culture is to clearly define the values and mission of the organization. This will ensure that everyone is working towards the same goals and will help to create a sense of purpose and direction. It is also important to communicate these values and mission to all employees, so that they understand the purpose of their work and how they contribute to the organization.

Effective communication is also crucial for developing a positive culture. Employees should be encouraged to share their ideas, opinions, and concerns, and management should be open to feedback. Clear, open, and honest communication helps to build trust and understanding among employees and can lead to more effective problem-solving and decision-making.

Another important aspect of developing a positive culture is to create a sense of community among employees. This can be achieved by promoting teamwork and collaboration, and encouraging employees to work together and support one another. Organizations can also foster a sense of community by hosting social events and encouraging employee involvement in volunteer or community service activities.

Another key aspect of developing a positive culture is to provide opportunities for employee development and growth. This can be achieved through training and development programs, as well as mentoring and coaching. By investing in the professional growth of employees, organizations can help to improve their skills and knowledge and increase job satisfaction.

It is also important to recognize and reward employees for their contributions. Acknowledge and appreciate the hard work and dedication of employees, and celebrate successes together. This will help to build morale and motivation among employees, and will encourage them to continue to work hard and strive for success.

It is important to lead by example and ensure that the organization's leaders embody the values and mission of the organization. This includes not only communicating the values but also living them and exemplifying them in actions. Developing a positive company culture is essential for the success of any organization. It requires clearly defined values and mission, effective communication, a sense of community, opportunities for employee development and growth, recognition and rewards for hard work and leaders who lead by example. By following these principles, organizations can create a positive and supportive work environment that will drive growth, innovation, and employee engagement.

*here are some tips for developing a positive company culture:*

**Clearly define the values and mission of the organization:** Communicate the values and mission of the organization to all employees and ensure that everyone understands the purpose of their work and how they contribute to the organization.

**Encourage open communication:** Encourage employees to share their ideas, opinions, and concerns, and be open to feedback. Clear, open and honest communication helps to build trust and understanding among employees.

**Promote teamwork and collaboration:** Create a sense of community among employees by promoting teamwork and collaboration and encouraging employees to work together and support one another.

**Provide opportunities for employee development and growth:** Invest in the professional growth of employees through training and development programs, mentoring, and coaching.

**Recognize and reward hard work:** Acknowledge and appreciate the contributions of employees and celebrate successes together.

**Lead by example:** Embody the values and mission of the organization and lead by example.

**Foster a sense of purpose:** Encourage employee engagement and job satisfaction by creating a sense of purpose and aligning employee's work with the organization's mission and values.

**Be open to change:** Be open to change and willing to adapt the culture as the organization evolves.

**Encourage work-life balance:** Provide flexible working hours or remote work options, when possible, which can help employees to better balance their work and personal lives.

**Listen to your employees:** Actively listen to the concerns and suggestions of employees, and take steps to address any issues that may be causing dissatisfaction.

A real-life example of a company with a positive company culture is the software company, SAS. SAS is known for its commitment to employee well-being and work-life balance. They provide their employees with a range of benefits such as on-site childcare, fitness centers and health clinics, and flexible working hours. Additionally, SAS has a culture of trust and empowerment, where employees are encouraged to take ownership of their roles and responsibilities. The company also provides opportunities for skill development and career growth, and has a reputation for promoting from within. This positive culture has helped SAS to attract and retain top talent, and has resulted in high employee satisfaction and engagement. SAS has been consistently ranked as one of the best places to work and is recognized for its positive company culture.

## Managing and motivating employees

Any organization's success depends on effective management and employee motivation. Growth, creativity, and productivity may all be fostered by a motivated and engaged team. It takes work, communication, and dedication from managers and leaders to effectively manage and inspire staff members.

The first step in managing and motivating employees is to set clear goals and expectations. This will ensure that everyone is working towards the same end goal and will prevent confusion and misunderstandings. It is also important to establish clear roles and responsibilities for each employee, so that they know what is expected of them and can work together more effectively.

Effective communication is also crucial for managing and motivating employees. Managers should be approachable and available to listen to the concerns and suggestions of employees. Clear, open, and honest communication helps to build trust and understanding among employees, and allows for more effective problem-solving and decision-making.

Another important aspect of managing and motivating employees is to provide opportunities for growth and development. This can be achieved through training and development programs, as well as mentoring and coaching. By investing in the professional growth of employees, managers can help to improve their skills and knowledge, which can lead to increased job satisfaction and improved performance.

Recognition and rewards for hard work are also important for motivating employees. Managers should acknowledge and appreciate the contributions of employees and celebrate successes together. This will help to build morale and motivation among employees, and will encourage them to continue to work hard and strive for success.

It is also important to lead by example and ensure that managers embody the values and mission of the organization. This includes not only communicating the values but also living them and exemplifying them in actions.

Managers should also create a positive and supportive work environment that encourages employee engagement and job satisfaction. This can be achieved by promoting teamwork and collaboration, and fostering a culture of open communication and mutual respect. It is important to be flexible and adaptable in managing and motivating employees. Different employees may have different motivations and needs, and managers should be willing to adjust their management style to meet these needs. Managing and motivating employees is essential for the success of any organization. It requires clear goals and expectations, effective communication, opportunities for growth and development, recognition and rewards for hard work, positive and supportive work environment, leadership by example and adaptability. By following these principles, managers can create a motivated and engaged workforce that will drive growth, innovation, and productivity.

*here are some tips for managing and motivating employees:*

**Set clear goals and expectations:** Clearly communicate the goals and objectives of the team or organization and ensure that everyone understands their role and responsibilities.

**Encourage open communication:** Encourage employees to share their ideas, opinions, and concerns and be open to feedback. Clear, open and honest communication helps to build trust and understanding among employees.

**Provide opportunities for growth and development:** Invest in the professional growth of employees through training and development programs, mentoring and coaching.

**Recognize and reward hard work:** Acknowledge and appreciate the contributions of employees and celebrate successes together.

**Lead by example:** Embody the values and mission of the organization and lead by example.

**Create a positive work environment:** Promote teamwork, collaboration and mutual respect and foster a culture of open communication.

**Be adaptable:** Different employees may have different motivations and needs, be willing to adjust your management style to meet these needs.

**Listen to your employees:** Actively listen to the concerns and suggestions of employees, and take steps to address any issues that may be causing dissatisfaction.

**Encourage work-life balance:** Provide flexible working hours or remote work options, when possible, which can help employees to better balance their work and personal lives.

**Provide meaningful incentives:** Provide incentives that are meaningful to the employees, such as bonuses, promotions, or additional benefits that align with their interests.

CHAPTER 4

# Marketing for Growth

**Marketing for Growth: Strategies for Small Businesses**

Marketing is the backbone of any successful business, and small businesses are no exception. In today's competitive marketplace, it's essential for small businesses to develop effective marketing strategies in order to attract and retain customers, increase brand awareness, and

ultimately drive growth. But with limited resources and a tight budget, it can be challenging for small businesses to create effective marketing campaigns that deliver results. One of the most important things to keep in mind when developing a marketing strategy is to understand your target audience. This means identifying the demographics of your ideal customer, including their age, gender, income, and interests. Once you have a clear picture of your target audience, you can tailor your marketing efforts to reach them more effectively.

One way to reach your target audience is through social media. Platforms like Facebook, Instagram, and Twitter are great tools for small businesses looking to connect with their customers. By creating engaging content, running social media promotions, and building a following on these platforms, small businesses can reach a large audience without spending a lot of money.

Another effective marketing strategy for small businesses is content marketing. This involves creating and sharing valuable and informative content with your target audience. This could be in the form of blog posts, videos, infographics, or other types of content that provide value to your customers. By providing helpful and informative content, small businesses can build trust and establish themselves as experts in their industry.

Search engine optimization (SEO) is another important marketing strategy for small businesses. This involves optimizing your website and online content to rank higher in search engine results, making it more likely that your target audience will find your business when searching for products or services related to your business. By implementing effective SEO strategies, small businesses can improve their visibility online and attract more customers to their website.

Email marketing is also a cost-effective way to reach your target audience. By building a list of email subscribers, small businesses can send targeted promotions and updates to their customers. This can help increase brand awareness and drive sales. It is also important to measure the results of your marketing efforts. By tracking metrics such as website traffic, social media engagement, and conversion rates, small businesses can determine which marketing strategies are working and which ones need to be improved.

Overall, marketing is essential for small businesses looking to drive growth and increase revenue. By understanding their target audience, using social media, content marketing, SEO, email marketing, and measuring the results, small businesses can create effective marketing campaigns that deliver results.

The best marketing strategy plan will vary depending on the specific industry, target audience, and goals of a business. However, a comprehensive marketing strategy plan generally includes the following elements:

**Market research:** Conduct research to understand your target audience, competitors, and industry trends. This will help you identify opportunities and challenges, and inform your marketing strategy.

**Goals and objectives:** Set clear and measurable goals and objectives that align with your overall business strategy. This will help you focus your efforts and track progress.

**Target audience:** Define your target audience in terms of demographics, psychographics, and behavior. This will help you create more effective messaging and campaigns.

**Branding:** Develop a strong brand identity and messaging that reflects your business's values and differentiates you from competitors.

**Marketing mix:** Determine the most effective marketing mix for your business, which could include a combination of the following:

- Product: Develop and improve your products or services to meet customer needs.
- Price: Set prices that are competitive and profitable.
- Place: Choose the best distribution channels to reach your target audience.

- Promotion: Develop a promotional plan that includes tactics such as advertising, public relations, sales promotions, and personal selling.

**Budget and metrics:** Establish a budget and metrics to measure the success of your marketing efforts. Make sure to track key performance indicators, such as website traffic, lead generation, and sales.

**Execution and adjustment:** Implement your marketing plan and monitor progress. Regularly evaluate the success of your efforts and make adjustments as needed.

**Building a strong brand**

Building a Strong Brand: The Importance of Branding for Small Businesses

Branding is a vital component of any successful business. A strong brand can differentiate a business from its competitors, create a sense of trust and loyalty among customers, and ultimately drive growth and revenue. However, for small businesses, building a strong brand can be a daunting task. With limited resources and a tight budget, it can be challenging to create a brand that stands out in a crowded marketplace.

One of the first steps in building a strong brand is to define your brand identity. This includes your brand's mission, values, and personality. This will help you establish a clear and consistent message that resonates with your target audience. A brand's mission statement should clearly communicate the purpose of the business, while values should reflect the fundamental beliefs that guide the business. A brand's personality should be able to reflect the company's culture, values and its positioning in the market.

Once you have a clear brand identity, it's important to create a consistent visual identity. This includes your logo, color scheme, and typography. Your visual identity should be simple and memorable, and should be used consistently across all marketing materials. A strong visual identity can help build brand recognition and make it easier for customers to identify your business.

Another important aspect of building a strong brand is to create valuable and consistent content. This can be in the form of blog posts, videos, infographics, or other types of content that provide value to your customers. By providing helpful and informative content, you can establish yourself as an expert in your industry and build trust with your target audience.

Social media is also a powerful tool for building a strong brand. Platforms like Facebook, Instagram, and Twitter are great ways to connect with customers and build a following. By creating engaging content and running social media promotions, small businesses can reach a large audience without spending a lot of money.

Customer service is also key in building a strong brand. By providing excellent customer service, you can create a positive customer experience and foster loyalty. This could include responding to customer inquiries and complaints in a timely manner, and going above and beyond to meet customer needs. It is important to measure the success of your branding efforts. By tracking metrics such as website traffic, social media engagement, and customer satisfaction, you can determine which strategies are working and which ones need to be improved. Building a strong brand is essential for small businesses looking to differentiate themselves from competitors, build trust and loyalty among customers, and ultimately drive growth and revenue. By defining their brand identity, creating a consistent visual identity, providing valuable and consistent content, leveraging social media, and measuring the success of their efforts, small businesses can create a brand that stands out in a crowded marketplace.

Dollar Shave Club, a company that disrupted the razor industry with its unique approach to branding. The company created a humorous and relatable brand voice that resonated with their target audience of young men. Their viral launch video, which featured the company's founder talking directly to the camera in a humorous and relatable manner, helped establish the brand's personality and quickly gained the attention of millions of viewers. Dollar Shave Club's strong brand and unique approach to marketing helped them grow from a small startup to a successful company that was eventually acquired by Unilever for $1 billion.

Another example of a company with a strong brand is Apple. Apple has built a reputation for creating high-quality, innovative products that are easy to use. The company's brand is synonymous with sleek design and cutting-edge technology. In addition to the quality of its products, Apple's branding strategy is characterized by simplicity and minimalism. The company's iconic logo, the minimalist aesthetic of its products and advertising campaigns all contribute to the company's strong brand image. Apple's brand is so strong that it has managed to create a loyal fan base, with many customers being willing to pay a premium for its products.

**Developing an effective marketing strategy**

Developing an effective marketing strategy is essential for any business looking to attract and retain customers, increase brand awareness, and ultimately drive growth. However, developing a marketing strategy can be a complex and time-consuming task, particularly for small businesses with limited resources and a tight budget. In this article, we will discuss some key steps that small businesses can take to develop an effective marketing strategy.

**Conduct Market Research:** The first step in developing a marketing strategy is to conduct market research. This includes understanding your target audience, competitors, and industry trends. This information will help you identify opportunities and challenges, and inform your marketing strategy.

**Set Clear Goals and Objectives:** Once you have a clear understanding of your target audience and the competitive landscape, you can set clear and measurable goals and objectives that align with your overall business strategy. This will help you focus your efforts and track progress.

**Define your Target Audience:** In order to develop an effective marketing strategy, it's important to understand your target audience in terms of demographics, psychographics, and behavior. This will help you create more effective messaging and campaigns that resonate with your target audience.

**Develop a Strong Brand Identity:** A strong brand identity can differentiate a business from its competitors and create a sense of trust and loyalty among customers. This includes creating a consistent visual identity, such as a logo, color scheme, and typography, as well as developing a clear and consistent brand message that reflects the values and mission of your business.

**Create a Marketing Mix:** Once you have a clear understanding of your target audience and a strong brand identity, you can determine the most effective marketing mix for your business. This could include a combination of product development, pricing strategy, distribution channels, and promotional tactics such as advertising, public relations, sales promotions, and personal selling.

**Establish a Budget and Metrics:** It's important to establish a budget for your marketing efforts and track metrics to measure the success of your strategies. This can include website traffic, lead generation, and sales.

**Implement and Adjust:** Once your marketing strategy is in place, it's important to implement it and monitor progress. Regularly evaluate the success of your efforts and make adjustments as needed.

creating a successful marketing strategy is crucial for small businesses seeking to draw in and keep clients, build brand recognition, and eventually spur growth. Small businesses can develop a marketing strategy that produces results by conducting market research, setting specific goals and objectives, identifying your target audience, developing a strong brand identity, developing a marketing mix, establishing a budget and metrics, and implementing and tweaking your strategy.

**Utilizing digital marketing to reach new customers**

Utilizing digital marketing to reach new customers is an effective and cost-efficient way for small businesses to expand their customer base. The rise of the internet and social media has created new opportunities for small businesses to reach a wider audience, and digital marketing provides a range of tools to do so. In this article, we will discuss some key strategies for small businesses to use digital marketing to reach new customers.

**Search Engine Optimization (SEO):** Optimizing your website for search engines can help improve your visibility online and attract more customers to your site. This includes optimizing your website's content, structure and meta tags to improve your search engine rankings. By creating quality content and using relevant keywords, small businesses can increase their chances of appearing on the first page of search engine results.

**Content Marketing:** Creating valuable and informative content can help attract new customers and build trust with your target audience. This can include blog posts, videos, infographics, and other types of content that provide value to your customers. By providing helpful and informative content, small businesses can establish themselves as experts in their industry and attract new customers.

**Social Media:** Social media platforms like Facebook, Instagram, and Twitter are great tools for small businesses to connect with their customers and reach a wider audience. By creating engaging content and running social media promotions, small businesses can reach a large audience without spending a lot of money.

**Email Marketing:** Email marketing is a cost-effective way to reach new customers. By building a list of email subscribers, small businesses can send targeted promotions and updates to their customers. This can help increase brand awareness and drive sales.

**Paid Advertising:** Paid advertising, such as Google AdWords or Facebook Ads, can help small businesses reach a larger audience and increase brand awareness. By targeting specific demographics and interests, small businesses can reach new customers who are more likely to be interested in their products or services.

**Mobile Optimization:** With the increasing use of mobile devices, it's important for small businesses to optimize their website for mobile devices. This includes using responsive design, which automatically adjusts the layout of the site to fit the screen size of the device, and reducing the amount of data that needs to be loaded to improve load time.

**Measuring and Optimizing:** It's important to measure the effectiveness of digital marketing efforts, such as website traffic, conversion rates and social media engagement, and adjust strategies to optimize results.

In conclusion, digital marketing provides small businesses with a range of tools to reach new customers. By using strategies such as search engine optimization, content marketing, social media, email marketing, paid advertising, mobile optimization, and measuring and optimizing efforts, small businesses can increase their visibility online and attract more customers to their business.

One real-life example of a small business utilizing digital marketing to reach new customers is the skincare company Glossier. The company was founded by a blogger and started as a small beauty blog, but over time it has grown into a successful e-commerce business. Glossier leveraged its following on social media platforms like Instagram and Twitter to build brand awareness and drive sales. They also used SEO and effective content marketing, such as blog post, videos and infographics, to attract new customers to their website. They also use email marketing to keep their customer engaged and offer personalized experience, which helps to build loyal customer base.

Another real-life example is a small bakery called "Georgetown Cupcake" which started as a small bakery in Washington D.C. but has grown into a successful nationwide business. They leveraged digital marketing strategies such as social media, email marketing, and paid advertising to reach new customers. They also used Instagram and other platforms to showcase their delicious cupcakes and attract new customers to their store. They also have an engaging website that has all the necessary information about the bakery and also allows customers to place orders online.

CHAPTER 5

# Financing for Growth

**Financing for Growth: Strategies for Small Businesses**

Small businesses face a unique set of challenges when it comes to financing their growth. With limited resources and a tight budget, it can be difficult for small businesses to secure the funding they need to expand their operations and increase revenue. In this article, we will discuss some of the most common financing options available to small businesses and strategies for securing the funding they need to grow

**Small Business Loans:** Small business loans are one of the most common financing options for small businesses. These loans are typically provided by banks and other lending institutions and can be used for a variety of purposes, such as purchasing equipment, hiring employees, or expanding operations. To qualify for a small business loan, businesses typically need to provide financial statements, tax returns, and a business plan.

**Crowdfunding:** Crowdfunding is a newer financing option that allows businesses to raise funds from a large number of people, usually via the internet. Crowdfunding can be a great option for small businesses that have a strong online presence, as it allows them to connect with potential investors and customers. Platforms like Kickstarter and Indiegogo allow small businesses to raise funds from a large number of people by offering rewards or equity in exchange for investment.

Angel Investors and Venture Capital: Angel investors and venture capital firms are another option for small businesses looking to raise growth capital. These investors typically provide funding in exchange for equity in the company. This can be a great option for small businesses that have a strong growth potential, but it can also be more difficult to secure funding from these investors.

**Government Grant**s: Small businesses may also be able to secure funding through government grants. These grants are typically provided by federal, state, and local governments and can be used for a variety of purposes, such as research and development, hiring employees, or expanding operations. To qualify for a government grant, businesses typically need to provide a detailed proposal and meet certain criteria.

**Business Credit Cards:** Business credit cards can also be a useful financing option for small businesses. These cards typically have higher credit limits than personal credit cards and offer rewards or cash back for business-related expenses. However, it's important for small businesses to be cautious when using credit cards to finance their growth, as high-interest rates and fees can make it difficult to repay the debt.

**Business Incubators:** Business incubators are organizations that provide small businesses with resources and support to help them grow. These resources can include office space, funding, and mentorship. Incubators can be a great option for small businesses that are just starting out or for those that are looking to scale up their operations.

There are several financing options available to small businesses looking to grow, including small business loans, crowdfunding, angel investors and venture capital, government grants, business credit cards, and business incubators. Each option has its own set of advantages and disadvantages, and it's important for small businesses to carefully consider their options and choose the best fit for their specific needs and goals.

**Understanding financing options**

Understanding Financing Options: A Guide for Small Businesses

As a small business owner, understanding the various financing options available to you is essential for making informed decisions about how to grow and sustain your business. From traditional bank loans to newer options like crowdfunding and angel investing, there are a wide range of options available to small businesses seeking funding. In this article, we will explore some of the most common financing options available to small businesses and provide guidance on how to evaluate and choose the best option for your business.

**Traditional Bank Loans:** Traditional bank loans, such as term loans and line of credit, are a common financing option for small businesses. These loans are typically provided by banks and other lending institutions and can be used for a variety of purposes, such as purchasing equipment, hiring employees, or expanding operations. To qualify for a traditional bank loan, small businesses typically need to have a strong credit history, provide financial statements and tax returns, and have a detailed business plan.

**Small Business Administration (SBA) Loans:** SBA loans are a type of loan program that is partially guaranteed by the Small Business Administration. These loans can be used for a variety of purposes, including working capital, inventory, and equipment. To qualify for an SBA loan, small businesses typically need to have a strong credit history, provide financial statements and tax returns, and have a detailed business plan.

**Crowdfunding:** Crowdfunding is a newer financing option that allows small businesses to raise funds from a large number of people, usually via the internet. Crowdfunding can be a great option for small businesses that have a strong online presence, as it allows them to connect with potential investors and customers. Platforms like Kickstarter and Indiegogo allow small businesses to raise funds by offering rewards or equity in exchange for investment.

**Angel Investors and Venture Capital:** Angel investors and venture capital firms are another option for small businesses looking to raise growth capital. These investors typically provide funding in exchange for equity in the company. This can be a great option for small businesses that have a strong growth potential, but it can also be more difficult to secure funding from these investors.

**Business Credit Cards:** Business credit cards can also be a useful financing option for small businesses. These cards typically have higher credit limits than personal credit cards and offer rewards or cash back for business-related expenses. However, it's important for small businesses to be cautious when using credit cards to finance their growth, as high-interest rates and

**Equipment Financing:** Equipment financing is a type of loan that allows small businesses to purchase equipment, such as machinery or vehicles, by making monthly payments over a period of time. This can be a great option for small businesses that need to purchase equipment to expand their operations, but don't have the cash on hand to make a large purchase upfront.

**Lease Financing:** Lease financing is another option for small businesses looking to purchase equipment. With lease financing, a business rents the equipment for a period of time, and at the end of the lease, the business has the option to purchase the equipment for a predetermined price. This can be a great option for small businesses that need to purchase equipment but don't have the cash on hand or don't want to tie up their cash in a large purchase.

**Invoice Financing:** Invoice financing is a type of loan that allows small businesses to borrow money based on their outstanding invoices. With invoice financing, a small business can borrow money against their unpaid invoices, and as the invoices are paid, the loan is repaid. This can be a great option for small businesses that have a lot of outstanding invoices but don't have the cash on hand to cover their expenses.

**Microloans:** Microloans are small loans that are typically provided by non-profit organizations or community-based lenders. These loans are designed for small businesses that might not qualify for traditional bank loans. Microloans can be used for a variety of purposes, such as working capital, inventory, and equipment.

there are a wide range of financing options available to small businesses, including traditional bank loans, SBA loans, crowdfunding, angel investors and venture capital, business credit

**Raising capital for growth**

Raising capital for growth is a crucial step for any business looking to expand and increase its market share. Whether you are a startup or an established company, having access to additional funds can help you take your business to the next level. In this article, we will explore the various ways in which businesses can raise capital for growth and the pros and cons of each method.

One of the most common ways to raise capital for growth is through equity financing. This is when a business issue shares of stock in exchange for cash. This is a popular option for startups, as it allows them to raise money without taking on debt. The main advantage of equity financing is that it does not require the business to pay back the money, but the downside is that it dilutes ownership and control among the existing shareholders.

Another way to raise capital for growth is through debt financing. This is when a business borrows money and agrees to pay it back with interest. Debt financing can take the form of loans from banks or other financial institutions, bonds, or other types of debt instruments. The main advantage of debt financing is that it does not dilute ownership and control, but the downside is that it requires the business to pay back the money with interest.

Crowdfunding is also becoming a popular way to raise capital for growth. This is when a business raises money from a large number of individuals, typically through an online platform. Crowdfunding can be a great option for startups, as it allows them to raise money from a wide range of people, including friends, family, and strangers. The main advantage of crowdfunding is that it allows for a large number of people to invest small amounts of money, but the downside is that it can be time-consuming and may not always be successful.

Another way to raise capital for growth is through angel investment. This is when a wealthy individual or group of individuals invest money in a business in exchange for an ownership stake. Angel investors can provide not only capital but also mentorship, guidance and networks to the business. The downside is that angel investors may want a significant ownership stake or a high level of control over the company's direction. businesses can also raise capital for growth by retaining earnings. This is when a business keeps a portion of its profits instead of distributing them to shareholders. Retained earnings can be used to invest in new equipment, research and development, or other growth opportunities. The main advantage of retaining earnings is that it does not dilute ownership or control and it does not require the business to pay back the money, but the downside is that it relies on the business generating profits.

There are many ways to raise capital for growth, each with its own advantages and disadvantages. The best method will depend on the specific circumstances of the business and its goals. Business owners should carefully consider all their options before making a decision and seek professional advice if needed.

Let's consider a fictional company called "Green Energy Inc." Green Energy Inc. is a solar panel manufacturing and installation company that has been in business for five years and has a strong reputation in the industry. The company is currently generating $10 million in annual revenue and has 20 employees. The management team has identified an opportunity to expand its offerings to include wind energy systems, but to do so, they will need to raise $5 million in additional capital.

*The management team has several options to raise capital for growth:*

**Equity Financing:** Green Energy Inc. could issue shares of stock in exchange for cash. This would allow them to raise $5 million in capital without taking on debt. However, this would also dilute the ownership and control of the existing shareholders.

**Debt Financing:** Green Energy Inc. could borrow $5 million from a bank or other financial institution and agree to pay it back with interest. This would not dilute the ownership and control of the existing shareholders, but the company would have to pay back the money with interest.

**Crowdfunding:** Green Energy Inc. could raise money from a large number of individuals through an online platform. This would allow them to raise $5 million in capital from a wide range of people, including friends, family, and strangers. However, it can be time-consuming and may not always be successful.

**Angel Investment:** Green Energy Inc. could raise $5 million from a wealthy individual or group of individuals in exchange for an ownership stake. This would provide not only capital but also mentorship, guidance and networks to the business. However, the angel investors may want a significant ownership stake or a high level of control over the company's direction.

**Retaining Earnings:** Green Energy Inc. could retain a portion of its profits instead of distributing them to shareholders to use for the expansion. This would not dilute the ownership and control of the existing shareholders and it does not require the business to pay back the money, but it relies on the business generating profits.

After considering all the options, the management team decides to go with a combination of equity financing and debt financing. They issue $2 million in new shares of stock to raise $2 million in capital, and borrow $3 million from a bank at a favorable interest rate. This allows them to raise the necessary $5 million in capital without diluting ownership and control too much, and also will be able to pay back the loan with the interest. With the additional capital, Green Energy Inc. is able to expand its offerings to include wind energy systems and grow its business.

**Managing financial risks**

Managing financial risks is an essential part of running a successful business. Financial risks are the potential threats to a company's financial well-being, such as loss of revenue, unexpected expenses, or market fluctuations. These risks can come from a variety of sources, including changes in the economy, natural disasters, and even the actions of competitors. To mitigate these risks, businesses must have a plan in place to identify, assess, and manage them.

One of the first steps in managing financial risks is identifying them. This involves looking at the company's operations, finances, and external factors that could potentially impact the business. For example, a company that relies heavily on a single customer or supplier may be at risk if that customer or supplier were to go out of business. A company that operates in a region prone to natural disasters may be at risk of damage to its physical assets. Identifying potential risks early on can help a business take preventative measures before they become major problems.

Once potential risks have been identified, the next step is to assess the likelihood of them occurring and the potential impact on the business. This will help the business prioritize which risks to focus on and allocate resources accordingly. For example, a risk that has a low likelihood of occurring but could have a significant impact on the business should be given a higher priority than a risk that has a higher likelihood of occurring but would have a minimal impact.

Once risks have been identified and assessed, the final step is to implement strategies to manage them. This can take many forms, including:

**Hedging:** This involves taking actions to offset potential losses, such as purchasing insurance or entering into financial contracts.

**Diversification:** By spreading investments or operations across multiple areas, a business can reduce its exposure to any one particular risk.

**Risk sharing:** this involves entering into partnership with other companies to share the risk and the potential benefit.

**Contingency planning:** Having a plan in place for how to respond in the event that a risk does occur can help a business minimize the damage.

**Monitoring and Reviewing:** Regularly monitoring and reviewing the risks and the effectiveness of the strategies put in place can help ensure that the business is always prepared for potential risks.

In conclusion, managing financial risks is an ongoing process that requires careful planning, monitoring and review. Businesses that take the time to identify, assess, and manage potential risks are better positioned to weather any financial storms that may arise. It is important to seek professional advice when needed and to keep in mind that the management of financial risks should be an integral part of the overall business strategy.

A retail business that relies heavily on foot traffic for sales may be at risk if there is a decrease in the number of people visiting the area. This could be due to a variety of factors, such as a new shopping center opening in a different part of town or a downturn in the local economy. In this case, the business could implement strategies to manage this risk such as diversifying their revenue streams by offering online sales and delivery options, offering discounts and promotions to attract customers, and investing in marketing to increase awareness of the business.

A manufacturing company that uses a single supplier for a key component of its products may be at risk if that supplier goes out of business or experiences a disruption in production. This could lead to a shortage of the component and disruptions in the company's production schedule. To manage this risk, the company could implement strategies such as diversifying its supplier base, building up inventory of the component, and creating a back-up plan in case the supplier is unable to deliver. Additionally, the company could establish a close relationship with the supplier, and having a good communication and coordination with them, could also help to mitigate the risk.

CHAPTER 6

# Managing Operations for Growth

Managing operations for growth is a critical aspect of any business. It involves identifying and implementing strategies to increase efficiency, productivity, and profitability in order to drive growth and expansion. In this article, we will explore some key strategies and best practices for managing operations for growth.

One of the most important strategies for managing operations for growth is to focus on process improvement. This involves identifying and streamlining key processes within the organization, such as production, logistics, and customer service. By identifying bottlenecks and inefficiencies, and implementing solutions to address them, businesses can improve overall productivity and efficiency, which in turn can drive growth.

Another key strategy for managing operations for growth is to invest in technology and automation. This can include everything from automation of manufacturing processes to the implementation of advanced logistics and inventory management systems. Automation can help to reduce labor costs, improve accuracy and precision, and increase overall productivity.

One of the most critical aspects of managing operations for growth is to focus on customer service. This includes providing excellent customer service, as well as identifying customer needs and preferences and working to meet them. By providing exceptional customer service, businesses can not only retain existing customers but also attract new ones, which can drive growth.

In addition, good communication is a vital part of managing operations for growth. This includes communication among employees, with customers, and with suppliers. Businesses that have clear, effective communication channels in place are better able to identify and address issues quickly, which can help to minimize disruptions and improve overall productivity.

Last but not least, it's critical to remember that managing operations for growth is a continuous process. To remain competitive and continue to spur growth, businesses must regularly analyze, assess, and change their processes.

Managing operations for growth is a critical aspect of any business. By focusing on process improvement, investing in technology and automation, providing excellent customer service, and maintaining effective communication, businesses can drive growth, increase efficiency, and improve overall profitability.

Here are some suggestions for running operations for expansion:

**Identify and streamline key processes:** Look for bottlenecks and inefficiencies in key processes such as production, logistics, and customer service. Implement solutions to address these issues and improve overall productivity and efficiency.

**Invest in technology and automation:** Automation can help to reduce labor costs, improve accuracy and precision, and increase overall productivity. Consider implementing advanced logistics and inventory management systems, as well as automation of manufacturing processes.

**Focus on customer service:** Providing excellent customer service is key to retaining existing customers and attracting new ones. Identify customer needs and preferences and work to meet them.

**Maintain effective communication:** Clear, effective communication channels are crucial for identifying and addressing issues quickly and minimizing disruptions.

**Continuously monitor and evaluate operations:** Managing operations for growth is an ongoing process. Continuously monitor and evaluate operations and make adjustments as needed to stay competitive and continue to drive growth.

**Prioritize Data-Driven Decisions:** Having access to accurate, real-time data can help you quickly identify areas of inefficiency and opportunities for optimization. It will also help you make data-driven decisions, which can lead to better long-term outcomes.

**Embrace Change:** Change is inevitable, especially in a rapidly evolving business environment. Embrace changes and be open to new ideas. Be prepared to pivot when necessary and be open to experimentation.

**Foster a Culture of Continuous Improvement:** Encourage your team to constantly look for ways to improve processes and systems. Create an environment where experimentation is encouraged and failure is seen as an opportunity for growth and learning.

**Build a Strong Team:** Having a strong, dedicated, and skilled team is essential for managing operations and driving growth. Invest in the development of your team members and provide them with the tools and resources they need to succeed.

**Leverage Supply Chain Management:** Optimizing your supply chain can help you reduce costs, improve efficiency, and increase responsiveness to customer demand. Invest in tools and technologies that can help you better manage and track your inventory, and develop strong relationships with your suppliers.

**Optimize Logistics:** Optimizing logistics can help you reduce transportation costs and improve delivery times. Invest in tools and technologies that can help you better track and manage your logistics, and work with partners to optimize your delivery routes.

**Implement Quality Management Systems:** Implementing quality management systems can help you ensure that your products and services meet the highest standards. Invest in tools and technologies that can help you track and manage quality, and provide your team with training on quality management best practices.

**Embrace Innovation:** Embrace new technologies, business models, and trends that can help you stay ahead of the competition and drive growth.

**Foster Collaboration:** Foster collaboration and communication among different departments and teams within your organization. This can help you identify and address issues more quickly, and also foster a culture of collaboration and innovation.

These recommendations can help firms run more efficiently and stimulate growth. It's crucial to be adaptable and agile since managing operations for development is a continual process that necessitates ongoing monitoring and review.

## Streamlining processes and systems

Streamlining processes and systems is an essential aspect of managing operations for growth. By identifying and addressing bottlenecks and inefficiencies in key processes, businesses can improve overall productivity, efficiency, and profitability, which in turn can drive growth and expansion. In this article, we will explore some best practices for streamlining processes and systems.

One of the most effective ways to streamline processes and systems is to conduct a thorough analysis of current operations. This involves identifying key processes and systems, and evaluating their effectiveness and efficiency. By identifying bottlenecks and inefficiencies, businesses can determine where improvements can be made and where resources can be better allocated.

Another key best practice for streamlining processes and systems is to implement process improvement methodologies such as Six Sigma or Lean Six Sigma. These methodologies are designed to help businesses identify and eliminate waste and improve overall efficiency. By training key employees in these methodologies and providing them with the tools and resources they need to succeed, businesses can improve the performance of their key processes and systems.

Another important aspect of streamlining processes and systems is to invest in technology and automation. Automation can help to reduce labor costs, improve accuracy and precision, and increase overall productivity. Businesses should consider implementing advanced logistics and inventory management systems, as well as automation of manufacturing processes.

In addition, it's important to communicate effectively with employees, customers, and suppliers. Clear, effective communication channels are crucial for identifying and addressing issues quickly and minimizing disruptions. Businesses that have a good communication strategy in place are better able to identify and address issues quickly and minimize disruptions.

To sum up, streamlining processes and systems is a critical aspect of managing operations for growth. By conducting a thorough analysis of current operations, implementing process improvement methodologies, investing in technology and automation, and maintaining effective communication, businesses can improve overall efficiency, productivity, and profitability, which in turn can drive growth and expansion. It's important to note that this is an ongoing process that requires continuous monitoring and evaluation, thus, businesses need to be flexible and adapt to changing conditions to achieve success.

## Implementing technology solutions

Implementing technology solutions is a key strategy for streamlining processes and systems. With the fast-paced technological advancements, businesses have access to a wide range of solutions that can help automate and optimize their operations.

One of the most popular technology solutions is enterprise resource planning (ERP) systems. These systems integrate and automate various business processes, such as accounting, inventory management, and customer relationship management. By implementing an ERP system, businesses can improve data visibility and accessibility, increase efficiency and productivity, and reduce operational costs.

Another technology solution that businesses can implement is a customer relationship management (CRM) system. These systems help businesses manage customer interactions and relationships, and can be used for marketing, sales, and customer service. A CRM system can help businesses improve customer service, increase sales and revenue, and gain a deeper understanding of customer needs and preferences.

Businesses can also implement automation solutions to streamline their manufacturing process. This can include robotic process automation (RPA) which is a form of software that can automate repetitive tasks across different systems and applications. Automation solutions can increase efficiency, reduce labor costs, and improve accuracy and precision.

Implementing technology solutions also includes investing in advanced analytics and business intelligence (BI) tools. These tools can help businesses make data-driven decisions by providing real-time insights into key performance indicators, such as sales, inventory, and customer behavior.

Firms can effectively streamline their systems and processes by utilizing technology solutions. Businesses can increase efficiency, productivity, and profitability by implementing ERP, CRM, automation, and sophisticated analytics, which can then spur growth and expansion. To ensure success, organizations must carefully consider the solution that best suits their objectives and have a well-defined deployment strategy.

*Here are some tips and examples for implementing technology solutions to streamline processes and systems:*

**Assess your business needs:** Before implementing any technology solutions, it's important to assess your business needs and identify which areas need the most improvement. This will help you determine which solutions will be the most beneficial for your organization.

**Research available solutions:** There are a wide variety of technology solutions available, so it's important to research and evaluate different options before making a decision. Consider factors such as cost, ease of use, and scalability when evaluating solutions.

**Create a clear implementation plan:** Once you have identified the solutions that will be most beneficial for your organization, it's important to create a clear implementation plan. This should include timelines, responsibilities, and clear objectives for the implementation.

**Provide training and support:** Implementing technology solutions can be a significant change for employees, so it's important to provide training and support to help them adjust. This can include training on how to use the new technology, as well as ongoing support to address any issues that may arise.

**Monitor and evaluate results:** After implementing technology solutions, it's important to monitor and evaluate the results. This can include tracking key performance indicators, such as productivity and efficiency, to determine whether the solutions are having the desired effect.

Examples of technology solutions that can be implemented to streamline processes and systems include:

- Implementing an ERP system to integrate and automate business processes such as accounting, inventory management, and customer relationship management
- Implementing a CRM system to manage customer interactions and relationships
- Automating manufacturing processes with robotic process automation (RPA)
- Investing in advanced analytics and BI tools to make data-driven decisions.

It's important to note that implementing technology solutions is an ongoing process, and businesses should continuously monitor and evaluate the results and make adjustments as needed to ensure success.

### Managing inventory and logistics

Managing inventory and logistics is a crucial aspect of streamlining processes and systems. Effective inventory and logistics management can help businesses reduce costs, improve efficiency, and increase responsiveness to customer demand. In this article, we will explore some best practices for managing inventory and logistics.

One of the most important aspects of managing inventory is to implement an inventory management system. These systems can help businesses track inventory levels, set reorder points, and generate reports on inventory movement. By having a clear view of inventory levels, businesses can ensure that they have the right products in stock to meet customer demand, and avoid stockouts or overstocking.

Another key aspect of managing inventory is to implement a just-in-time (JIT) inventory system. JIT systems are designed to minimize inventory levels by ordering products only as they are needed. This can help businesses reduce inventory costs, and also improve efficiency by reducing the amount of time and resources required to manage inventory.

Managing logistics is also a critical aspect of streamlining processes and systems. This includes everything from optimizing delivery routes to implementing advanced logistics and tracking systems. By optimizing logistics, businesses can reduce transportation costs and improve delivery times.

Effective communication with partners and suppliers is also crucial. Channels of communication that are clear and efficient are essential for reducing disruptions, rapidly recognizing problems, and dealing with them. Businesses are better equipped to manage inventories and logistics and reduce interruptions when they have excellent ties with their partners and suppliers.

Lastly but not least, it's critical to remember that managing inventory and logistics is a continuous process. To remain competitive and continue to spur growth, businesses must regularly analyze, assess, and change their processes.

Controlling inventory and logistics is a key component of optimizing systems and processes. Businesses can lower costs, boost efficiency, and improve response to consumer demand by using inventory management systems, JIT inventory systems, optimizing logistics, and maintaining excellent communication with suppliers and partners. This can support their growth and ability to compete.

*Below are some pointers for handling logistics and inventory:*

**Implement an inventory management system:** Inventory management systems can help businesses track inventory levels, set reorder points, and generate reports on inventory movement. This can help businesses ensure they have the right products in stock to meet customer demand and avoid stockouts or overstocking.

**Implement a just-in-time (JIT) inventory system:** JIT systems are designed to minimize inventory levels by ordering products only as they are needed. This can help businesses reduce inventory costs and improve efficiency by reducing the amount of time and resources required to manage inventory.

**Optimize logistics:** Optimizing logistics can help businesses reduce transportation costs and improve delivery times. This includes everything from optimizing delivery routes to implementing advanced logistics and tracking systems.

**Communicate effectively with suppliers and partners:** Clear, effective communication channels are crucial for identifying and addressing issues quickly and minimizing disruptions. Businesses that have strong relationships with their suppliers and partners are better able to manage inventory and logistics, and also minimize disruptions.

**Continuously monitor and evaluate inventory and logistics:** Managing inventory and logistics is an ongoing process. Continuously monitor and evaluate operations and make adjustments as needed to stay competitive and continue to drive growth.

**Prioritize Data-Driven Decisions:** Having access to accurate, real-time data can help you quickly identify areas of inefficiency and opportunities for optimization. It will also help you make data-driven decisions, which can lead to better long-term outcomes.

**Automate where possible:** Automation can help to reduce labor costs, improve accuracy and precision, and increase overall productivity. Consider automating tasks such as inventory tracking, reordering, and logistics tracking.

**Foster a Culture of Continuous Improvement:** Encourage your team to constantly look for ways to improve inventory and logistics processes and systems. Create an environment where experimentation is encouraged and failure is seen as an opportunity for growth and learning.

Zara is a great example of effective inventory and logistics management is Zara, a Spanish clothing and accessories retailer. The company has implemented a unique business model known as fast fashion, which allows them to quickly design, produce, and deliver new clothing styles to market. They use an agile supply chain management system, where they continuously monitor trends and customer demand, and quickly adjust their production accordingly. This allows them to keep inventory low and produce only what is needed, reducing waste and costs. Additionally, they have a quick turnaround time on production and delivery, which allows them to meet the fast-changing fashion trends.

Dell is another great example of effective inventory and logistics management. The company has implemented a direct-to-consumer sales model, which allows them to build computers and other electronics to order, reducing the need for large amounts of inventory. They also use advanced logistics systems to optimize delivery routes and minimize transportation costs. Additionally, Dell has implemented a just-in-time (JIT) inventory system, which allows them to minimize inventory levels and reduce costs. The company also utilizes automation in their logistics and inventory management processes, which has helped them to improve efficiency and reduce labor costs.

These examples show how businesses can implement effective inventory and logistics management strategies to improve efficiency, reduce costs, and increase responsiveness to customer demand. These companies have implemented sophisticated systems and processes, and they continuously monitor and evaluate their operations to adapt to changing conditions. By following their examples, businesses can improve their inventory and logistics management, which can help to drive growth and expansion.

CHAPTER 7

# Managing Growth Challenges

"Managing Growth Challenges" refers to the process of addressing the obstacles and difficulties that can arise as a business or organization experiences growth.

As a company grows, it may face a variety of challenges such as increasing competition, changing market conditions, and the need to expand or restructure operations. These challenges can have a significant impact on the company's ability to continue growing and achieving its goals.

Effective management of growth challenges involves identifying the specific issues that are impacting the company, developing strategies to address those issues, and implementing those strategies in a timely and efficient manner. This may involve changes to the company's business model, organizational structure, or overall approach to operations.

It may also involve investing in new technologies or resources, such as marketing and sales automation tools, or hiring additional staff with specialized skills. Additionally, it may also involve collaboration with other companies, partners or organizations to share knowledge, resources, and develop new opportunities.

Managing growth challenges also involves effectively communicating with stakeholders, including employees, customers,

shareholders, and suppliers. Clear and effective communication can help to ensure that everyone is aware of the challenges the company is facing and understands the steps being taken to address them.

Another important aspect of managing growth challenges is monitoring and measuring the effectiveness of the strategies and actions taken. This includes regularly assessing the company's performance and progress towards its goals, and making any necessary adjustments or course corrections.

It's also important to have a robust financial management system in place to manage the growth challenges. This includes monitoring cash flow and ensuring that the company has sufficient funding to support its growth, as well as developing financial projections and budgeting to anticipate and plan for future expenses.

Managing growth challenges also requires leadership and decision-making skills. The company's leaders must be able to make difficult decisions and take calculated risks in order to navigate the challenges and capitalize on opportunities. It is a difficult process that needs a combination of strategic thought, strong leadership, good communication, and financial management. It's a continuous effort that calls for adaptability to shifting circumstances, flexibility, and a willingness to take calculated risks in order to succeed.

*The following advice can help you deal with growing challenges:*

**Identify the specific challenges you are facing:** Understand the specific obstacles that are impacting your company's ability to grow.

This will help you to develop targeted strategies to address those challenges.

**Develop a comprehensive growth plan:** Create a plan that outlines the steps your company will take to achieve its goals. This plan should include strategies to address specific challenges, as well as a timeline for implementing those strategies.

**Communicate effectively with stakeholders:** Keep employees, customers, shareholders, and suppliers informed about the challenges your company is facing and the steps being taken to address them. Clear and effective communication can help to ensure that everyone is on the same page.

**Monitor and measure performance:** Regularly assess your company's performance and progress towards its goals. This will help you to make any necessary adjustments or course corrections.

**Invest in new technologies and resources:** Consider investing in new technologies or resources that can help your company to be more efficient and effective. This might include marketing and sales automation tools, or hiring additional staff with specialized skills.

**Collaborate with others:** Collaborate with other companies, partners or organizations to share knowledge, resources, and develop new opportunities.

**Be flexible and adaptable:** Be prepared to adapt to changing conditions and opportunities. This may require making difficult decisions and taking calculated risks.

**Have a robust financial management system in place:** Monitor cash flow and ensure that the company has sufficient funding to support its growth. Also, develop financial projections and budgeting to anticipate and plan for future expenses.

**Strong leadership is key:** The company's leaders must be able to make difficult decisions and take calculated risks in order to navigate the challenges and capitalize on opportunities.

**Prioritize customer satisfaction:** Keep your customers at the center of your business strategy. Make sure you understand their needs and tailor your products/services to meet those needs. This will help to increase customer loyalty and retention.

**Monitor industry trends:** Keep an eye on industry trends and changes in the market. This will help you to anticipate and respond to challenges more effectively.

**Empower your employees:** Give your employees the autonomy and resources they need to make decisions and take action. This will help to create a culture of ownership and accountability, which is essential for managing growth challenges.

**Focus on scalability:** As your business grows, it's important to have systems and processes in place that can scale with it. This will help to ensure that your company can continue to operate efficiently and effectively as it grows.

**Develop a risk management plan:** Identify potential risks and develop a plan to mitigate them. This will help to protect your company from potential losses and minimize the impact of challenges.

**Stay agile:** Be prepared to pivot or change direction if your current strategies are not working. Be open to new ideas and approaches and be willing to experiment with different solutions.

**Continuously evaluate and improve:** Continuously evaluate your growth strategies and processes, and make adjustments as needed. This will help to ensure that your company is always operating at its best.

It's crucial to keep in mind that handling growth issues calls for a variety of tactics, strong leadership, and efficient communication. You may overcome the difficulties and seize the opportunities that come with growth by heeding the advice in this article and being ready to change course when necessary.

Simulating a growth challenge scenario can be an effective way to prepare for and manage potential challenges in the future. Here's an example of how a growth simulation might work:

1. Identify a specific growth challenge scenario: For example, imagine your company has experienced rapid growth and is now facing increased competition in the market.
2. Assemble a team: Bring together a cross-functional team of employees with relevant expertise, such as marketing, operations, and finance.
3. Develop a simulation plan: The team should develop a plan that simulates the scenario, including the specific challenges and obstacles the company will face, as well as potential strategies and solutions.
4. Run the simulation: The team should run the simulation, role-playing different aspects of the scenario and testing different strategies and solutions.
5. Evaluate and debrief: After the simulation is complete, the team should evaluate the results, identifying any successes and areas for improvement. They should also debrief to discuss what they learned, and how they can apply that knowledge to real-world challenges.

6. Develop a plan of action: Based on the simulation, the team should develop a plan of action that outlines specific steps the company can take to address the challenges they simulated.

7. Implement and monitor: Implement the plan of action, monitor progress and make necessary adjustments.

It's vital to remember that this is only an illustration and that the particulars of the simulation will rely on the difficulties your organization is now experiencing. The simulation's objective is to give the team a secure and controlled environment where they can test out various approaches and solutions and develop a deeper understanding of the difficulties they may encounter.

One real-life example of a company managing growth challenges is the ride-sharing company Uber.

In the early days of the company, Uber experienced rapid growth as it expanded to cities around the world. However, as the company grew, it faced a number of challenges such as increasing competition from other ride-sharing companies, regulatory hurdles, and safety concerns.

To address these challenges, Uber developed a number of strategies such as:

- Investing in new technologies, such as self-driving cars and a range of transportation options

- Expanding into new markets, such as food delivery and electric bike rentals

- Improving safety measures, such as mandatory background checks for drivers and in-app emergency assistance

- Collaborating with cities and governments to address regulatory concerns

Uber also communicated effectively with stakeholders, such as its customers, drivers and partners, and provided them with the necessary information and support to navigate the challenges.

In order to better concentrate on its core business and enhance its financial performance, Uber's management team also made a number of modifications to the company's organizational structure and leadership responsibilities.

Ultimately, Uber's management team successfully navigated the difficulties of expansion by pinpointing the particular problems they were experiencing, creating focused plans to address those concerns, and swiftly and efficiently putting those strategies into practice.

## Dealing with unexpected obstacles

Dealing with unexpected obstacles is a common challenge for companies experiencing growth. These obstacles can include things like changes in the market, unexpected competition, or unforeseen regulatory changes.

One way to deal with unexpected obstacles is to have a flexible and adaptable approach to business operations. This means being willing to pivot or change direction if current strategies are not working. It's important to be open to new ideas and approaches, and to be willing to experiment with different solutions.

Another important strategy is to have a robust risk management plan in place. This means identifying potential risks and developing a plan to mitigate them. This will help to protect your company from potential losses and minimize the impact of unexpected obstacles.

Effective communication and collaboration are also key. Keep your employees, customers, shareholders and suppliers informed about the situation and the steps that are being taken to address the obstacle. This will help to ensure that everyone is on the same page and working towards a common goal.

Last but not least, it's critical to have a capable leadership group in place. To overcome unforeseen challenges and seize opportunities, the company's leaders must be able to make difficult choices and take measured risks. Overcoming unforeseen challenges necessitates a combination of adaptability, flexibility, risk management, good communication, and strong leadership. A corporation must continually make an effort to be ready for the unexpected and to react rapidly to opportunities and changing market conditions. Continually make an effort to be ready for the unexpected and to react rapidly to opportunities and changing market conditions.

*Here are some tips for dealing with unexpected obstacles:*

8. Remain calm and composed: When faced with unexpected obstacles, it's important to remain calm and composed. This will help you to think clearly and make informed decisions.

9. Assess the situation: Take a step back and assess the situation. Understand the nature of the obstacle and the impact it's having on your business.

10. Identify potential solutions: Brainstorm potential solutions to the obstacle. Think creatively and don't be afraid to consider unconventional options.

11. Prioritize and select the best solution: Evaluate the potential solutions and prioritize the most effective and feasible options.

12. Communicate and collaborate: Keep employees, customers, shareholders, and suppliers informed about the situation and the

steps that are being taken to address the obstacle. Collaborate with other companies, partners, or organizations to share knowledge, resources, and develop new opportunities.

13. Implement and monitor: Implement the chosen solution and monitor progress. Be prepared to make adjustments as needed.

14. Learn from the experience: Use the obstacle as an opportunity to learn and improve for the future. Identify what worked well and what didn't, and make adjustments accordingly.

15. Be proactive: Be proactive in identifying potential obstacles and risks that may arise in the future. This will help you to be better prepared to deal with unexpected challenges.

16. Have a plan B: Always have a plan B, a backup plan in case the first plan doesn't work out as expected.

17. Have a strong leadership team: The company's leaders must be able to make difficult decisions and take calculated risks in order to navigate the unexpected obstacles and capitalize on opportunities.

The Moroccan Automotive Industry: The Moroccan automotive industry is a significant contributor to the country's economy and has experienced significant growth in recent years. However, the industry has faced unexpected obstacles such as the global economic downturn, which has led to a decrease in demand for cars. To address this obstacle, the Moroccan government implemented a series of measures to support the industry, such as tax exemptions for car manufacturers and the development of new investment opportunities in the industry. Additionally, the government has also invested in the development of new technologies, such as electric and hybrid vehicles, to diversify the industry and make it more resilient to future economic challenges.

The Moroccan Solar Energy Industry: Morocco has set a goal to produce 42% of its electricity from renewable sources by 2020. The country's solar energy industry has experienced significant growth in recent years, with the development of large-scale solar power plants. However, the industry has faced unexpected obstacles such as the fluctuation of international prices of raw materials and the lack of trained human resources. To address these obstacles, the Moroccan government has implemented a series of measures such as investing in the training of local engineers and technicians, as well as incentivizing the use of local raw materials in the production of solar panels. Additionally, the government has also signed agreements with international partners to share knowledge and expertise in the field of solar energy, to further develop the industry.

**Adapting to change**

Adapting to change is an essential skill for individuals, organizations, and societies. The world is constantly changing and the ability to adapt is essential for survival and success. Change can come in many forms, such as technological advancements, changes in the economy, shifts in social norms, or unexpected events.

For individuals, adapting to change can mean finding a new job, relocating to a new city, or dealing with a personal loss. For organizations, it can mean implementing new technologies, changing business models, or responding to shifting market conditions. And for societies, it can mean adapting to new laws and regulations, dealing with natural disasters, or addressing issues of social and economic inequality.

*Adapting to change requires several key elements:*

**Recognizing the need for change:** The first step in adapting to change is recognizing that a change is necessary. This can be difficult, as we often feel comfortable in our current circumstances and may be resistant to change. However, understanding the implications of not making that change can help motivate us to take action.

**Being open-minded:** Being open to new ideas and perspectives is essential for adapting to change. We need to be willing to consider different options and be open to new ways of doing things. This requires a mindset of curiosity and a willingness to learn.

**Being proactive:** Anticipating and preparing for potential changes is important. Rather than waiting for change to happen, we should be proactive and look for ways to stay ahead of the curve. This can mean investing in new technologies, diversifying our skill sets, or looking for new opportunities.

**Being flexible and resilient:** Adapting to change requires flexibility and resilience. We need to be able to quickly adjust to new circumstances and bounce back from setbacks. This can be challenging, but with the right mindset and approach, it is possible to develop these skills.

**Embracing learning:** Continuous learning is a key aspect of adapting to change. We need to seek out new information and experiences in order to improve our skills and knowledge. This requires a commitment to lifelong learning and a willingness to take risks.

Adapting to change is not always easy, but with the right mindset and approach, it can be an opportunity for growth and development. It can help us to become more resilient, more creative, and more adaptable. And it can help us to navigate the challenges and opportunities of an ever-changing world.

It is crucial to be proactive, open-minded, adaptable, and resilient in order to successfully traverse the process of adapting to change. Accepting new knowledge and constantly looking for fresh experiences can also be quite beneficial for adapting to change. It's crucial to recognize that while change can be challenging and painful, it can also present an opportunity for personal growth and development if handled correctly.

Netflix is an actual case study of a business adjusting to change.

In the early days of the company, Netflix was primarily a DVD-by-mail rental service. However, as technology and consumer behavior changed, the company recognized the need to adapt. With the rise of streaming technology and the increasing popularity of on-demand video, Netflix realized that the future of home entertainment was moving away from physical media.

To adapt to this change, Netflix shifted its focus to streaming. The company invested in developing its own streaming technology, and began producing its own original content. This allowed Netflix to differentiate itself from its competitors and remain relevant in the rapidly changing media landscape.

Additionally, Netflix also adopted a data-driven approach, using data and analytics to understand its customers' preferences, and tailor its content and recommendations accordingly. This helped the company to better understand its customers and offer them a more personalized experience.

As a result of these changes, Netflix has become one of the most successful and innovative companies in the media industry. It's now one of the largest streaming services in the world, and its original content has won numerous awards and accolades.

Overall, Netflix's ability to adapt to change has been key to its success. The company recognized the need to change, was open-minded to new opportunities and embraced learning, and was able to pivot its strategy and business model to stay relevant in the rapidly evolving media landscape.

### Managing stress and burnout

Stress and burnout are increasingly common problems in today's fast-paced world. Stress is the body's response to challenging or demanding situations and it's normal to experience stress from time to time. But when stress becomes chronic and overwhelming, it can lead to burnout. Burnout is a state of physical, emotional, and mental exhaustion caused by prolonged and excessive stress.

Managing stress and burnout is important for maintaining overall health and well-being. Stress and burnout can have negative effects on mental and physical health, and can impact work performance and personal relationships.

*Here are some tips for managing stress and burnout:*

**Prioritize self-care:** Self-care is essential for managing stress and burnout. Make time for activities that promote physical and mental well-being, such as exercise, healthy eating, and getting enough sleep. It's important to take care of yourself, both physically and emotionally.

**Practice mindfulness:** Mindfulness techniques, such as meditation and deep breathing, can help to reduce stress and improve mental well-being. Mindfulness can help you to focus on the present moment, rather than dwelling on the past or worrying about the future.

**Set boundaries:** Learn to say no to non-essential commitments and set limits on your workload. It's important to set boundaries for yourself and protect your time and energy.

**Connect with others:** Maintaining social connections and support networks can help to reduce stress and promote a sense of well-being. Talking to friends and family, or seeking support from a therapist or counselor, can help to provide a sense of perspective and understanding.

**Take breaks:** Regularly taking short breaks throughout the day can help to reduce stress and improve productivity. It's important to step away from work and other demands and give yourself a chance to recharge.

**Seek professional help:** If stress and burnout are impacting your well-being and ability to function, consider seeking professional help from a counselor or therapist. A professional can help you to develop strategies for managing stress and burnout and can provide support and guidance.

**Prioritize activities that you enjoy:** Make time for hobbies and activities that you enjoy and that bring you joy. Engaging in activities that you enjoy can help to reduce stress and promote a sense of well-being.

**Have realistic expectations:** Don't put too much pressure on yourself to achieve unrealistic goals. Instead, set realistic expectations for yourself and focus on progress, not perfection.

**Be proactive:** Identify potential stressors and develop strategies to manage them before they lead to burnout. This can include things like time management techniques, delegating tasks, and setting boundaries. By being proactive, you can anticipate and manage stress before it becomes overwhelming.

**Take care of your physical health:** Regular exercise, healthy eating, and adequate sleep can all help to reduce stress and improve overall health. Taking care of your physical health can also help to improve your mental and emotional well-being.

It's vital to keep in mind that managing stress and burnout calls for a combination of self-care, mindfulness, and social support. It's crucial to recognize that everyone has different pressures and coping processes, and that what works for one person might not work for another. It's important to strike a balance that suits your needs and your way of life.

Burnout and stress are widespread issues in today's fast-paced society. It's crucial to act in order to control stress and avoid burnout. You can learn to manage stress and lower the risk of burnout by prioritizing self-care, practicing mindfulness, setting boundaries, connecting with others, taking breaks, seeking professional help, prioritizing activities you enjoy, having realistic expectations, being proactive, and taking care of your physical health. Keep in mind that managing stress and burnout calls for a combination of self-care, mindfulness, and social support.

One example of a historical figure from Islamic history who adapted to change and managed stress and burnout is Umar ibn Al-Khattab. He was a companion of the Prophet Muhammad and the second Caliph of the Islamic empire.

Umar was known for his strong leadership skills and his ability to adapt to changing circumstances. He was appointed as Caliph during a time of great turmoil in the empire, following the death of the Prophet Muhammad. However, he was able to lead the empire through a period of rapid expansion and consolidation. He was able to make difficult decisions and take calculated risks to navigate the empire through the difficult times.

Umar also managed stress and burnout by prioritizing self-care, connecting with others and seeking counsel from his advisors. He was known for his humility and ability to listen to others. He would often seek the advice of the companions of the Prophet and other leaders, which helped him to make better decisions and manage the empire effectively.

Umar was known for his commitment to justice and fairness, which helped to reduce stress and burnout among the people. He implemented policies that ensured that the needs of the poor and marginalized were met, and he worked to create a society that was just and equitable for all. Umar's ability to adapt to change, manage stress and burnout, and implement policies that promoted justice and fairness helped him to be a successful leader during a time of great change and turmoil in Islamic history.

CHAPTER 8

# Case Studies

Case studies are in-depth examination of a particular situation or event, often used as a method of teaching or research. They can provide detailed information on how an individual, organization, or society has adapted to change, and how they have managed stress and burnout.

One example of a case study on adapting to change is the case of Kodak. Kodak was a leading company in the photography industry, but with the advent of digital technology, it failed to adapt and as a result, it filed for bankruptcy in 2012. The case study examines how Kodak's failure to adapt to the changing technology landscape led to its decline, and how it could have taken steps to remain competitive.

Another example of a case study on managing stress and burnout is the case of a nurse working in a hospital emergency department. This case study examines the high levels of stress and burnout experienced by nurses working in this demanding environment, and the steps that the hospital has taken to address these issues, including offering counseling and support services, and implementing more flexible scheduling.

Case studies can be found in various sources such as academic journals, business publications and online platforms. They can be useful in providing detailed and real-life examples of how individuals, organizations, or societies have adapted to change and managed stress and burnout, and can provide valuable insights and lessons for others facing similar challenges.

**Success stories of small businesses that have achieved**

One example of a small business that has achieved significant growth from France is Nuxe. Nuxe is a French skincare and cosmetics company that was founded in 1989. The company specializes in natural and organic skincare products and has gained a reputation for its high-quality and innovative products.

To achieve significant growth, Nuxe adapted to changing consumer preferences by focusing on natural and organic ingredients, and investing in research and development to create new and innovative products. The company also implemented a strong distribution strategy, which included partnerships with leading retailers, such as Sephora, and expanded to international markets.

Nuxe also leveraged digital marketing, such as social media and influencer partnerships, to reach and engage with customers. They also created an e-commerce platform to sell their products directly to customers.

As a result of these changes, Nuxe has grown rapidly and today it's considered one of the leading skincare and cosmetics companies in France. The company has a strong presence in more than 60 countries and has a wide range of products.

Another example is Withings, which is a French company that specializes in connected health devices. Founded in 2008, Withings quickly gained popularity for its innovative and user-friendly products, such as connected scales and blood pressure monitors.

To achieve significant growth, Withings adapted to the changing consumer preferences by focusing on the connected health market, and investing in research and development to create new and innovative products. The company also implemented a strong distribution strategy, which included partnerships with leading retailers, such as Amazon, and expanded to international markets.

Withings also leveraged digital marketing, such as social media and influencer partnerships, to reach and engage with customers. They also created an e-commerce platform to sell their products directly to customers.

As a result of these changes, Withings has grown rapidly and today it's considered one of the leading companies in the connected health market. The company was acquired by Nokia in 2016 and has continued to innovate and expand its product line.

These are a few examples of small businesses from France that have achieved significant growth by adapting to change and leveraging new opportunities. They recognized the need to change, embraced learning, and implemented new strategies to reach and engage with customers.

From the examples of Nuxe and Withings, there are several lessons that can be learned about achieving significant growth for small businesses:

**Lessons learned from their experiences**

**Adapt to changing consumer preferences:** Both Nuxe and Withings recognized that consumer preferences were changing and adapted their products and business models accordingly. Nuxe focused on natural and organic ingredients, and Withings focused on the connected health market. By adapting to changing consumer preferences, these companies were able to remain relevant and attract new customers.

**Invest in research and development:** Both Nuxe and Withings invested in research and development to create new and innovative products. This helped them to stand out from the competition and attract customers with unique and high-quality offerings.

**Implement a strong distribution strategy:** Both Nuxe and Withings implemented a strong distribution strategy, which included partnerships with leading retailers, such as Sephora and Amazon, and expansion to international markets. This helped them to reach a wider audience and increase their revenue.

**Leverage digital marketing:** Both Nuxe and Withings leveraged digital marketing, such as social media and influencer partnerships, to reach and engage with customers. They also created e-commerce platforms to sell their products directly to customers. This helped them to reach a wider audience and increase their revenue.

**Be willing to take risks and try new things:** Both Nuxe and Withings were willing to take risks and try new things. They recognized that change is a constant in business and that in order to grow, they needed to be open to new opportunities and be willing to adapt.

**Build a strong brand:** Both Nuxe and Withings have built strong brands that are associated with high-quality and innovative products. A strong brand can help to attract customers, differentiate a business from its competitors, and increase customer loyalty.

**Have a clear vision and mission:** Both Nuxe and Withings have a clear vision and mission that guides their business decisions and strategies. Having a clear vision and mission can help a business to stay focused, aligned, and motivated towards achieving its goals.

**Prioritize customer service and satisfaction:** Both Nuxe and Withings prioritize customer service and satisfaction, which helps them to build a loyal customer base and positive reputation. By providing excellent customer service, businesses can increase customer retention, improve customer loyalty and satisfaction, and attract new customers through positive word-of-mouth.

**Continuously monitor the market:** Both Nuxe and Withings continuously monitor the market and adjust their strategies accordingly. By keeping an eye on industry trends, competitors, and customer feedback, businesses can identify potential challenges and opportunities, and make informed decisions that will help them to grow.

**Be open to collaborations and partnerships:** Both Nuxe and Withings have benefited from collaborations and partnerships with other companies and organizations. By working with others, businesses can access new resources, expertise, and networks that can help them to achieve their goals.

Small firms can improve their chances of attaining considerable growth and set themselves up for long-term success by applying these lessons. These guidelines are applicable to all small enterprises globally, not only those in France.

**Conclusion**

In conclusion, growing a small business is a challenging but rewarding endeavor that requires a combination of strategy, planning, execution, and adaptability. Achieving significant growth is essential for the survival and success of small businesses, and it can bring many benefits, such as increased revenue, market share, and competitiveness.

The process of growing a small business can be divided into several key areas: assessing your business's growth potential, developing a growth plan, building a strong team, marketing for growth, financing for growth, managing operations for growth, and managing growth challenges.

Assessing your business's growth potential involves identifying your business's current stage, analyzing your industry and competition, and identifying opportunities for growth. Developing a growth plan involves setting measurable growth goals, identifying the resources required for growth, and prioritizing and implementing growth initiatives.

Building a strong team is crucial for growing a small business. This includes hiring and retaining top talent, developing a positive company culture, and managing and motivating employees. Marketing for growth involves building a strong brand, developing an effective marketing strategy, and utilizing digital marketing to reach new customers.

Financing for growth involves understanding financing options, raising capital for growth, and managing financial risks. Managing operations for growth involves streamlining processes and systems, implementing technology solutions, and managing inventory and logistics. Managing growth challenges involves dealing with unexpected obstacles, adapting to change, and managing stress and burnout.

The success stories of small businesses that have achieved significant growth can provide valuable insights and lessons for other small businesses facing similar challenges. These case studies demonstrate the importance of adapting to change, prioritizing and implementing growth initiatives, building a strong brand, and having a clear vision and mission.

Growing a small business requires a combination of strategy, planning, execution, and adaptability. By following the key takeaways and recommendations outlined in this book, small business owners can increase their chances of achieving significant growth and long-term success. It's important to remember that the process of growing a small business is ongoing, and requires continuous monitoring, learning, and adaptation.

## Summarizing the key takeaways

*The key takeaways from this book on small business growth are:*

- Small business growth is important for the survival and success of a company and its stakeholders.
- Growing a small business requires a combination of strategy, planning, execution, and adaptability.
- Assessing a business's growth potential, developing a growth plan, building a strong team, marketing for growth, financing for growth, managing operations for growth and managing growth challenges are key areas to consider when trying to grow a small business.
- Adapting to change, prioritizing and implementing growth initiatives, building a strong brand, having a clear vision and mission, and continuously monitoring the market are essential for achieving significant growth.

- Case studies of small businesses that have achieved significant growth can provide valuable insights and lessons for other small businesses facing similar challenges.
- Financing options and managing financial risks are also important to consider when trying to grow a small business.
- The process of growing a small business is ongoing, and requires continuous monitoring, learning, and adaptation.
- Providing excellent customer service, improving customer loyalty and satisfaction, and attracting new customers through positive word-of-mouth is important
- Leveraging digital marketing, and utilizing technology solutions can also be effective in reaching and engaging customers
- Building a strong team, developing a positive company culture, and managing and motivating employees are crucial for growing a small business.

## Final thoughts and recommendations

In terms of final thoughts, it is important to remember that growing a small business is a challenging but rewarding endeavor that requires hard work, dedication, and perseverance. There is no one-size-fits-all solution for small business growth, and each business will have its own unique set of challenges and opportunities.

However, by following the key takeaways and recommendations outlined in this book, small business owners can increase their chances of achieving significant growth and long-term success. It is important to be open to change, continuously monitor the market, and be willing to adapt and try new things.

In terms of recommendations, small business owners should:

- Assess their business's growth potential and identify opportunities for growth.
- Develop a growth plan that includes measurable goals, resources required, and growth initiatives.
- Build a strong team by hiring and retaining top talent, developing a positive company culture, and managing and motivating employees.

- Implement an effective marketing strategy, build a strong brand, and utilize digital marketing to reach new customers.
- Seek financing options and manage financial risks.
- Streamline processes and systems, implement technology solutions, and manage inventory and logistics to manage operations for growth.
- Be prepared to deal with unexpected obstacles and adapt to change.
- Monitor industry trends, competitors, and customer feedback to make informed decisions
- Prioritize customer service and satisfaction to build a loyal customer base and positive reputation.
- Consider collaborations and partnerships with other companies and organizations to access new resources, expertise, and networks that can help them to achieve their goals.

Small business entrepreneurs can improve their chances of experiencing considerable growth and long-term success by adhering to these suggestions

e author,

...I Bouttan, a highly accomplished individual with a wealth of ...ige and experience in both academia and industry. A graduate from the prestigious University of Marrakech with a degree in business management, Imad has built a successful career as the founder of Zorna Furniture, a company that has made a name for itself in the furniture industry in Morocco. With a keen eye for design, a deep understanding of website development and a natural talent for leadership, Imad is a true visionary in the world of business.

This book's author has a wealth of experience in creating effective networks and building strong relationships, which has been a key factor in the success of Zorna Furniture. He has always been passionate about helping other small business owners achieve their goals and has been a mentor and advisor to many. In this book, [Your Name] shares their invaluable insights and experience to help guide you on your own journey to success. Whether you're just starting out or looking to take your business to the next level, Imad provides practical and actionable advice to help you reach your goals. This book is a must-read for anyone looking to achieve sustainable growth for their small business. "

www.ingramcontent.com/pod-product-compliance
Lightning Source LLC
Chambersburg PA
CBHW050004230526
45465CB00003BB/1257